Andrew Linn,
Emmanuel College,
Cambridge 1988

New Accents

General Editor: TERENCE HAWKES

TRANSLATION STUDIES

IN THE SAME SERIES

Structuralism and Semiotics   *Terence Hawkes* *
Linguistics and the Novel   *Roger Fowler*
Reading Television   *John Fiske and John Hartley*
Subculture: The Meaning of Style   *Dick Hebdige*
Formalism and Marxism   *Tony Bennett*
Critical Practice   *Catherine Belsey*
Science Fiction: Its Criticism and Teaching   *Patrick Parrinder*
The Semiotics of Theatre and Drama   *Keir Elam*
Fantasy: The Literature of Subversion   *Rosemary Jackson*
Sexual Fiction   *Maurice Charney*
Re-Reading English   *ed. Peter Widdowson*
Deconstruction: Theory and Practice   *Christopher Norris*
Orality and Literacy   *Walter J. Ong*
Poetry as Discourse   *Antony Easthope*
Literature and Propaganda   *A. P. Foulkes*
Narrative Fiction   *Shlomith Rimmon-Kenan*
Reception Theory   *Robert C. Holub*
Psychoanalytic Criticism: Theory in Practice   *Elizabeth Wright*
Metafiction: The Theory and Practice of Self-conscious
    Fiction   *Patricia Waugh*
Alternative Shakespeares   *ed. John Drakakis*
Making a Difference: Feminist Literary Criticism
    ed. Gayle Greene and Coppélia Kahn
Rewriting English: Cultural Politics of Gender and Class
    Janet Batsleer, Tony Davies, Rebecca O'Rourke and Chris Weedon
The Unusable Past: Theory and the Study of American
    Literature   *Russell J. Reising*
Literature, Politics and Theory: Papers from the Essex Conference
    1976–1984   *ed. Francis Barker, Peter Hulme, Diana Loxley and
    Margaret Iversen*
Popular Fictions: Essays in Literature and History
    ed. Peter Widdowson, Peter Humm and Paul Stigant
Criticism in Society   *Imre Salusinszky*
The Return of the Reader: Reader-response Criticism   *Elizabeth
    Freund*
Superstructuralism: The Philosophy of Structuralism and
    Poststructuralism   *Richard Harland*

* Not available from Methuen, Inc. in the USA

SUSAN BASSNETT-McGUIRE

TRANSLATION STUDIES

METHUEN
LONDON AND NEW YORK

First published in 1980 by
Methuen & Co. Ltd
11 New Fetter Lane, London EC4P 4EE
Reprinted twice
Reprinted 1987

Published in the USA by
Methuen & Co.
in association with Methuen, Inc.
29 West 35th Street, New York, NY 10001

Printed in Great Britain by
Richard Clay (The Chaucer Press) Ltd
Bungay, Suffolk

British Library Cataloguing in Publication Data

Bassnett-McGuire, Susan
    Translation studies – (New accents).
    1. Translating and interpreting
    I. Title   II. Series
    418'.02   P306   80-41069

    ISBN 0-416-72870-7
    ISBN 0-416-72880-4 Pbk

For my father, who made it all possible.

CONTENTS

General Editor's Preface   ix
Acknowledgements   xi

INTRODUCTION   1

1   CENTRAL ISSUES   13

Language and culture   13
Types of translation   14
Decoding and recoding   16
Problems of equivalence   23
Loss and gain   30
Untranslatability   32
Science or 'secondary activity'?   37

2   HISTORY OF TRANSLATION THEORY   39

Problems of 'period study'   40
The Romans   43
Bible translation   45
Education and the vernacular   50
Early theorists   53
The Renaissance   55
The seventeenth century   58
The eighteenth century   61
Romanticism   64
Post-Romanticism   67
The Victorians   68
Archaizing   72
The twentieth century   73

3   SPECIFIC PROBLEMS OF LITERARY TRANSLATION   76

Structures   76
Poetry and translation   81
Translating prose   109

Translating dramatic texts   120

CONCLUSION   133

Notes   136
Select bibliography   147
Appendix: The original text of The Seafarer   153
Index   156

GENERAL EDITOR'S PREFACE

I T is easy to see that we are living in a time of rapid and radical social change. It is much less easy to grasp the fact that such change will inevitably affect the nature of those academic disciplines that both reflect our society and help to shape it.

Yet this is nowhere more apparent than in the central field of what may, in general terms, be called literary studies. Here, among large numbers of students at all levels of education, the erosion of the assumptions and presuppositions that support the literary disciplines in their conventional form has proved fundamental. Modes and categories inherited from the past no longer seem to fit the reality experienced by a new generation.

New Accents is intended as a positive response to the initiative offered by such a situation. Each volume in the series will seek to encourage rather than resist the process of change, to stretch rather than reinforce the boundaries that currently define literature and its academic study.

Some important areas of interest immediately present themselves. In various parts of the world, new methods of analysis have been developed whose conslusions reveal the limitations of the Anglo-American outlook we inherit. New concepts of literary forms and modes have been proposed;

new notions of the nature of literature itself, and of how it communicates are current; new views of literature's role in relation to society flourish. *New Accents* will aim to expound and comment upon the most notable of these.

In the broad field of the study of human communication, more and more emphasis has been placed upon the nature and function of the new electronic media. *New Accents* will try to identify and discuss the challenge these offer to our traditional modes of critical response.

The same interest in communication suggests that the series should also concern itself with those wider anthropological and sociological areas of investigation which have begun to involve scrutiny of the nature of art itself and of its relation to our whole way of life. And this will ultimately require attention to be focused on some of those activities which in our society have hitherto been excluded realignment of values involved and the disconcerting nature of the pressures that work to bring it about both constitute areas that *New Accents* will seek to explore.

Finally, as its title suggests, one aspect of *New Accents* will be firmly located in contemporary approaches to language, and a continuing concern of the series will be to examine the extent to which relevant branches of linguistic studies can illuminate specific literary areas. The volumes with this particular interest will nevertheless presume no prior technical knowledge on the part of their readers, and will aim to rehearse the linguistics appropriate to the matter in hand, rather than to embark on general theoretical matters.

Each volume in the series will attempt an objective exposition of significant developments in its field up to the present as well as an account of its author's own views of the matter. Each will culminate in an informative bibliography as a guide to further study. And while each will be primarily concerned with matters relevant to its own specific interests, we can hope that a kind of conversation will be heard to develop between them: one whose accents may perhaps suggest the distinctive discourse of the future.

TERENCE HAWKES

ACKNOWLEDGEMENTS

THIS book grew out of several years' work with post-graduate students at the University of Warwick. I should like to thank all my students past and present for their invaluable help. I am grateful also to those friends and colleagues engaged in practical and theoretical translation work, most especially to Paul Merchant and Tony Phelan of the University of Warwick, Drummond Bone of the University of Glasgow, Professor Albrecht Neubert of Karl Marx University, Leipzig and to the Leuven/Amsterdam group for many hours of valuable discussion. My thanks are due also to the British Academy whose assistance made it possible for me to work in the German Democratic Republic and in Czechoslovakia in researching this book.

I am particularly grateful to my colleagues Clive Barker and Jennifer Lorch of the University of Warwick who read and commented on sections of the manuscript in its early stages and also to Marijane Osborn of the University of Hawaii. Thanks also to Christine Wyman for typing the manuscript. Finally, I should like to express my gratitude to the staff of the University of Warwick crèche and to Stella Dixon, without whom I would not have had the physical time in which to write at all.

The author and publishers would like to thank the following individuals and companies for granting permission to reproduce material for this book:

E.J. Brill, Leiden, for the diagram taken from Eugene Nida's *Towards a Science of Translating*, 1964; MIT Press, Cambridge, Mass., for the diagram from B.L. Whorf, *Language Thought and Relativity*, 1956; Oxford University Press for Charles Kennedy's translation of *The Seafarer* taken from *An Anthology of Old English Poetry* (New York, 1960) and also for Sir William Marris's translation of Catullus Poem 13, first published in 1924; University of Michigan Press, Ann Arbor, for Frank Copley's translation of Catullus Poem 13, first published in 1957; Arnold Mondadori for Ungaretti's poem *Un'altra notte* and for the passage from Silone's *Fontamara*; *Stand* for Charles Tomlinson's translation and Penguin Books Ltd for P. Creagh's translation of Ungaretti's poem; Journeyman Press for G. David and E. Mossbacher's translation of Silone's *Fontamara*; S. Fischer-Verlag, Frankfurt-am-Main for the passage from Mann's *Der Zauberberg*; Martin Secker & Warburg Ltd and Alfred A. Knopf, Inc. for H.T. Lowe-Porter's translation of Mann's *The Magic Mountain*; Faber and Faber Ltd for Robert Lowell's translation of *Phaedra* and Ezra Pound's *The Seafarer* from *The Translations of Ezra Pound*; Tony Harrison and Rex Collings, London, for Tony Harrison's *Phaedra Brittanica*.

INTRODUCTION

I N 1978, in a brief Appendix to the collected papers of the 1976 Louvain Colloquium on Literature and Translation, André Lefevere proposed that the name *Translation Studies* should be adopted for the discipline that concerns itself with 'the problems raised by the production and description of translations'.[1] The present book is an attempt to outline the scope of that discipline, to give some indication of the kind of work that has been done so far and to suggest directions in which further research is needed. Most importantly, it is an attempt to demonstrate that Translation Studies is indeed a discipline in its own right: not merely a minor branch of comparative literary study, nor yet a specific area of linguistics, but a vastly complex field with many far-reaching ramifications.

The relatively recent acceptance of the term Translation Studies may perhaps surprise those who had always assumed that such a discipline existed already in view of the widespread use of the term 'translation', particularly in the process of foreign language learning. But in fact the systematic study of translation is still in swaddling bands. Precisely because translation is perceived as an intrinsic part of the foreign language teaching process, it has rarely been studied for its own sake.

What is generally understood as translation involves the rendering of a source language (SL) text[2] into the target language (TL) so as to ensure that (1) the surface meaning of the two will be approximately similar and (2) the structures of the SL will be preserved as closely as possible but not so closely that the TL structures will be seriously distorted. The instructor can then hope to measure the students' linguistic competence, by means of the TL product. But there the matter stops. The stress throughout is on understanding the syntax of the language being studied and on using translation as a means of demonstrating that understanding.

It is hardly surprising that such a restricted concept of translation goes hand in hand with the low status accorded to the translator and to distinctions usually being made between the writer and the translator to the detriment of the latter. Hilaire Belloc summed up the problem of status in his Taylorian lecture *On Translation* as long ago as 1931, and his words are still perfectly applicable today:

> The art of translation is a subsidiary art and derivative. On this account it has never been granted the dignity of original work, and has suffered too much in the general judgement of letters. This natural underestimation of its value has had the bad practical effect of lowering the standard demanded, and in some periods has almost destroyed the art altogether. The corresponding misunderstanding of its character has added to its degradation: neither its importance nor its difficulty has been grasped.[3]

Translation has been perceived as a secondary activity, as a 'mechanical' rather than a 'creative' process, within the competence of anyone with a basic grounding in a language other than their own; in short, as a low status occupation. Discussion of translation products has all too often tended to be on a low level too; studies purporting to discuss translation 'scientifically' are often little more than idiosyncratic value judgements of randomly selected translations of the work of major writers such as Homer, Rilke, Baudelaire or Shakespeare. What is analysed in such studies is the *product* only, the end result of the translation process and not the process itself.

The powerful Anglo-Saxon anti-theoretical tradition has proved especially unfortunate with regard to Translation Studies, for it has merged so aptly with the legacy of the 'servant-translator' that arose in the English-speaking world in the nineteenth century. In the eighteenth century there had been a number of studies on the theory and practice of translation in various European languages, and 1791 had seen the publication of the first theoretical essay on translation in English, Alexander Tytler's *Essay on the Principles of Translation* (see pp. 63–4). But although in the early nineteenth century translation was still regarded as a serious and useful method for helping a writer explore and shape his own native style, much as it had been for centuries, there was also a shift in the status of the translator, with an increasing number of 'amateur' translators (amongst whom many British diplomats) whose object in translating had more to do with circulating the contents of a given work than with exploring the formal properties of the text. Changing concepts of nationalism and national languages marked out intercultural barriers with increasing sharpness, and the translator came gradually to be seen not as a creative artist but as an element in a master-servant relationship with the SL text.[4] Hence Dante Gabriel Rossetti could declare in 1861 that the work of the translator involved self-denial and repression of his own creative impulses, suggesting that

> often would he avail himself of any special grace of his own idiom and epoch, if only his will belonged to him; often would some cadence serve him but for his author's structure – some structure but for his author's cadence . . .[5]

At the opposite extreme Edward Fitzgerald, writing about Persian poetry in 1851, could state 'It is an amusement to me to take what liberties I like with these Persians, who, (as I think) are not Poets enough to frighten one from such excursions, and who really do want a little Art to shape them.'[6]

These two positions, the one establishing a hierarchical relationship in which the SL author acts as a feudal overlord exacting fealty from the translator, the other establishing a hierarchical relationship in which the translator is absolved from all responsibility to the inferior culture of the SL text are both quite consistent with the growth of colonial imperialism in the nineteenth century. From these positions derives the ambiguity with which translations have come to be regarded in the twentieth century. For if translation is perceived as a servile occupation, it is unlikely to be dignified by analysis of the techniques utilized by the servant, and if translation is seen as the pragmatic activity of an individual with a mission to 'upgrade' the SL text, an analysis of the translation process would cut right across the established hierarchical system.

Further evidence of the conflicting attitudes towards translation in the English-speaking world can be drawn from the way in which educational systems have come to rely increasingly on the use of translated texts in teaching, without ever attempting to study the processes of translation. Hence a growing number of British or North American students read Greek and Latin authors in translation or study major nineteenth-century prose works or twentieth-century theatre texts whilst treating the translated text as if it were originally written in their own language. This is indeed the greatest irony of the whole translation debate: that those very scholars who reject the need to investigate translation scientifically because of its traditional low status in the academic world do at the same time teach a substantial number of translated texts to monolingual students.

The nineteenth-century legacy has also meant that translation study in English has devoted much time to the problem of finding a term to describe translation itself. Some scholars, such as Theodore Savory,[7] define translation as an 'art'; others, such as Eric Jacobsen,[8] define it as a 'craft'; whilst others, perhaps more sensibly, borrow from the German and describe it as a 'science'.[9] Horst Frenz[10] even goes so far as to opt for 'art' but with qualifications, claiming that 'translation is neither a creative art nor an imitative art, but stands somewhere between the two.' This emphasis on terminological debate in English points again to the problematic of English Translation Studies, in which a value system underlies the choice of term. 'Craft' would imply a slightly lower status than 'art' and carry with it suggestions of amateurishness, while 'science' could hint at a mechanistic approach and detract from the notion that translation is a creative process. At all events, the pursual of such a debate is purposeless and can only draw attention away from the central problem of finding a terminology that can be utilized in the systematic study of translation. So far, in English, only one attempt has been made to tackle the terminological issue, with the publication in 1976 of Anton Popovič's *Dictionary for the Analysis of Literary Translation*:[11] a work that sets out, albeit in skeletal form, the basis of a methodology for studying translation.

Since the early 1960s significant changes have taken place in the field of Translation Studies, with the growing acceptance of the study of linguistics and stylistics within literary criticism that has led to developments in critical methodology and also with the rediscovery of the work of the Russian Formalist Circle. The most important advances in Translation Studies in the twentieth century derive from the groundwork done by groups in Russia in the 1920s and subsequently by the Prague Linguistic Circle and its disciples. Vološinov's work on Marxism and philosophy, Mukařovský's on the semiotics of art, Jakobson, Prochazka and Levý on translation (see Section 3) have all established new criteria for the founding of a theory of translation and have showed that, far from being a dilettante pursuit accessible to anyone with a minimal knowledge of another language, translation is, as Randolph Quirk puts it, 'one of the most difficult tasks that a writer can take upon himself.'[12] That translation involves far more than a working acquaintance with two languages is aptly summed up by Levý, when he declares that

> A translation is not a monistic composition, but an interpenetration and conglomerate of two structures. On the

one hand there are the semantic content and the formal contour of the original, on the other hand the entire system of aesthetic features bound up with the language of the translation.[13]

The stress on linguistics and the early experiments with machine translation in the 1950s led to the rapid development of Translation Studies in Eastern Europe, but the discipline was slower to emerge in the English-speaking world. J.C. Catford's short study in 1965 tackled the problem of linguistic untranslatability (see pp. 32–7) and suggested that

> In *translation*, there is substitution of TL meanings for SL meanings: not transference of TL meanings into the SL. In *transference* there is an implantation of SL meanings into the TL text. These two processes must be clearly differentiated in any theory of translation.[14]

He thus opened a new stage of the debate on translation in English. But although his theory is important for the linguist, it is nevertheless restricted in that it implies a narrow theory of meaning. Discussion of the key concepts of equivalence and cultural untranslatability (see Section 1) has moved on a long way since his book first appeared.

Since 1965, great progress has been made in Translation Studies. The work of scholars in the Netherlands, Israel, Czechoslovakia, the Soviet Union, the German Democratic Republic and the United States seems to indicate the emergence of clearly defined schools of Translation Studies, which place their emphasis on different aspects of the whole vast field. Moreover, translation specialists have benefited a great deal from work in marginally related areas. The work of Italian and Soviet semioticians, developments in grammatology and narratology, advances in the study of bilingualism and multilingualism and child language-learning can all be utilized within Translation Studies.

Translation Studies, therefore, is exploring new ground, bridging as it does the gap between the vast area of stylistics, literary history, linguistics, semiotics and aesthetics. But at the same time it must not be forgotten that this is a discipline firmly rooted in practical application. When André Lefevere tried to define the goal of Translation Studies he suggested that its purpose was to 'produce a comprehensive theory which can also be used as a guideline for the production of translations',[15] and whilst some may question the specificity of this statement, his clear intention to link theory with practice is indisputable. The need for systematic study of translation arises directly from the problems encountered during the actual translation process and it is as essential for those working in the field to bring their practical experience to theoretical discussion, as it is for increased theoretical perceptiveness to be put to use in the translation of texts. To divorce the theory from the practice, to set the scholar against the practitioner as has happened in other disciplines, would be tragic indeed.

Although Translation Studies covers such a wide field, it can be roughly divided into four general areas of interest, each with a degree of overlap. Two are *product-oriented*, in that the emphasis is on the functional aspects of the TL text in relation to the SL text, and two of them are *process-oriented*, in that the emphasis is on analysing what actually takes place during translation.

The first category involves the *History of Translation* and is a component part of literary history. The type of work involved in this area includes investigation of the theories of translation at different times, the critical response to translations, the practical processes of commissioning and publishing translations, the role and function of translations in a given period, the methodological development of translation and, by far the most common type of study, analysis of the work of individual translators.

The second category, *Translation in the TL culture*, extends the work on single texts or authors and includes work on the influence of a text, author or genre, on the absorption of the norms of the translated text into the TL system and on the principles of selection operating within that system.

The third category *Translation and Linguistics* includes

studies which place their emphasis on the comparative arrangement of linguistic elements between the SL and the TL text with regard to phonemic, morphemic, lexical, syntagmatic and syntactic levels. Into this category come studies of the problems of linguistic equivalence, of language-bound meaning, of linguistic untranslatability, of machine translation, etc. and also studies of the translation problems of non-literary texts.

The fourth category, loosely called *Translation and Poetics*, includes the whole area of literary translation, in theory and practice. Studies may be general or genre-specific, including investigation of the particular problems of translating poetry, theatre texts or libretti and the affiliated problem of translation for the cinema, whether dubbing or sub-titling. Under this category also come studies of the poetics of individual translators and comparisons between them, studies of the problems of formulating a poetics, and studies of the inter-relationship between SL and TL texts and author-translator-reader. Above all in this section come studies attempting to formulate a theory of literary translation.

It would be fair to say that work in categories 1 and 3 is more widespread than work in categories 2 and 4, although there is little systematic study of translation history and some of the work on translation and linguistics is rather isolated from the mainstream of translation study. It is important for the student of translation to be mindful of the four general categories, even while investigating one specific area of interest, in order to avoid fragmentation.

There is, of course, one final great stumbling block waiting for the person with an interest in Translation Studies: the question of *evaluation*. For if a translator perceives his or her role as partly that of 'improving' either the SL text or existing translations, and that is indeed often the reason why we undertake translations, an implicit value judgement underlies this position. All too often, in discussing their work, translators avoid analysis of their own methods and concentrate on exposing the frailties of other translators. Critics, on the other hand, frequently evaluate a translation from one or other of two limited standpoints: from the narrow view of the closeness of the translation to the SL text (an evaluation that can only be made if the critic has access to both languages) or from the treatment of the TL text as a work in their own language. And whilst this latter position clearly has some validity — it is, after all, important that a play should be playable and a poem should be readable – the arrogant way in which critics will define a translation as good or bad from a purely monolingual position again indicates the peculiar position occupied by translation *vis-à-vis* another type of *metatext* (a work derived from, or containing another existing text), literary criticism itself.

In his famous reply to Matthew Arnold's attack on his translation of Homer, Francis Newman declared that

> Scholars are the tribunal of Erudition, but of Taste the educated but unlearned public is the only rightful judge; and to it I wish to appeal. Even scholars collectively have no right, and much less have single scholars, to pronounce a final sentence on questions of taste in their court.[16]

Newman is making a distinction here between evaluation based on purely academic criteria and evaluation based on other elements, and in so doing he is making the point that assessment is *culture bound*. It is pointless, therefore, to argue for a definitive translation, since translation is intimately tied up with the context in which it is made. In his useful book *Translating Poetry, Seven Strategies and a Blueprint*,[17] André Lefevere compares translations of Catullus' Poem 64 with a view not to comparative evaluation but in order to show the difficulties and at times advantages of a particular method. For there is no universal canon according to which texts may be assessed. There are whole sets of canons that shift and change and each text is involved in a continuing dialectical relationship with those sets. There can no more be the ultimate translation than there can be the ultimate poem or the ultimate novel, and any assessment of a translation can only be made by taking into account both the process of creating it and its function in a given context.

As will be illustrated later in this book, the criteria for the translation process and the function of the TL text have varied enormously through the ages. The nineteenth-century English concern with reproducing 'period flavour' by the use of archaisms in translated texts, often caused the TL text to be more inaccessible to the reader than the SL text itself. In contrast, the seventeenth-century French propensity to gallicize the Greeks even down to details of furniture and clothing was a tendency that German translators reacted to with violent opposition. Chapman's energetic Renaissance Homer is far removed from Pope's controlled, masterly eighteenth-century version. Yet to compare the two with a view to evaluating them in a hierarchical structure would serve no purpose.

The problem of evaluation in translation is intimately connected with the previously discussed problem of the low status of translation, which enables critics to make pronouncements about translated texts from a position of assumed superiority. The growth of Translation Studies as a discipline, however, should go some way towards raising the level of discussion about translations, and if there are criteria to be established for the evaluation of a translation, those criteria will be established from within the discipline and not from without.

In the present book, the problem of evaluation is not developed at any length, partly due to reasons of space but mainly because the purpose of this book is to set out the basics of the discipline rather than to offer a personal theory. The book is organized in three sections, in an attempt to present as many aspects of the field of Translation Studies as possible. Section 1 is concerned with the central issues of translation, with the problem of *meaning, untranslatability* and *equivalence*, and with the question of translation as a part of communication theory. Section 2 traces lines through different time periods, to show how concepts of translation have differed through the ages and yet have been bound by common links. Section 3 examines the specific problems of translating poetry, prose and drama. The emphasis throughout is on *literary translation*, although some of the issues discussed in Section 1 are applicable to all aspects of translation and interpreting.

I am well aware that among the many aspects of translation not developed here, the problem of translation between non-related languages is clearly one of the most crucial. This aspect of translation is considered briefly in Section 1, but since to my great regret I am only able to work in Indo-European languages, I thought it best not to venture into areas outside my competence, except where points of general theoretical principle are concerned that might be applicable to all languages.

Underlying this discussion of translation is the belief that there *are* general principles of the process of translation that can be determined and categorized, and, ultimately, utilized in the cycle of text — theory — text regardless of the languages involved.

1 CENTRAL ISSUES

Language and culture

THE first step towards an examination of the processes of translation must be to accept that although translation has a central core of linguistic activity, it belongs most properly to *semiotics*, the science that studies sign systems or structures, sign processes and sign functions (Hawkes, *Structuralism and Semiotics,* London 1977). Beyond the notion stressed by the narrowly linguistic approach, that translation involves the transfer of 'meaning' contained in one set of language signs into another set of language signs through competent use of the dictionary and grammar, the process involves a whole set of extra-linguistic criteria also.

Edward Sapir claims that 'language is a guide to social reality' and that human beings are at the mercy of the language that has become the medium of expression for their society. Experience, he asserts, is largely determined by the language habits of the community, and each separate structure represents a separate reality:

> No two languages are ever sufficiently similar to be considered as representing the same social reality. The worlds in which different societies live are distinct worlds, not merely the same world with different labels attached.[1]

Sapir's thesis, endorsed later by Benjamin Lee Whorf, is related to the more recent view advanced by the Soviet semiotician, Jurí Lotman, that language is a *modelling system*. Lotman describes literature and art in general as *secondary modelling systems*, as an indication of the fact that they are derived from the primary modelling system of language, and declares as firmly as Sapir or Whorf that 'No language can exist unless it is steeped in the context of culture; and no culture can exist which does not have at its center, the structure of natural language.'[2] Language, then, is the heart within the body of culture, and it is the interaction between the two that results in the continuation of life-energy. In the same way that the surgeon, operating on the heart, cannot neglect the body that surrounds it, so the translator treats the text in isolation from the culture at his peril.

Types of translation

In his article 'On Linguistic Aspects of Translation', Roman Jakobson distinguishes three types of translation:[3]

(1) Intralingual translation, or *rewording* (an interpretation of verbal signs by means of other signs in the same language).

(2) Interlingual translation or *translation proper* (an interpretation of verbal signs by means of some other language).

(3) Intersemiotic translation or *transmutation* (an interpretation of verbal signs by means of signs of nonverbal sign systems).

Having established these three types, of which (2) *translation proper* describes the process of transfer from SL to TL, Jakobson goes on immediately to point to the central problem in all types: that while messages may serve as adequate interpretations of code units or messages, there is ordinarily no full equivalence through translation. Even apparent synonymy does not yield equivalence, and Jakobson shows how intralingual translation often has to resort to a combination of code units in order to <u>fully</u> interpret the meaning of a single unit. Hence a dictionary of so-called synonyms may give *perfect* as a synonym for *ideal* or *vehicle* as a synonym for *conveyance* but in neither case can there be said to be complete equivalence, since each unit contains within itself a set of non-transferable associations and connotations.

Because complete equivalence (in the sense of synonymy or sameness) cannot take place in any of his categories, Jakobson declares that all poetic art is therefore technically untranslatable:

> Only creative transposition is possible: either intralingual transposition – from one poetic shape into another, or interlingual transposition – from one language into another, or finally intersemiotic transposition – from one system of signs into another, e.g. from verbal art into music, dance, cinema or painting.

What Jakobson is saying here is taken up again by Georges Mounin, the French theorist, who perceives translation as a series of operations of which the starting point and the end product are *significations* and function within a given culture.[4] So, for example, the English word *pastry*, if translated into Italian without regard for its signification, will not be able to perform its function of meaning within a sentence, even though there may be a dictionary 'equivalent'; for *pasta* has a completely different associative field. In this case the translator has to resort to a combination of units in order to find an approximate equivalent. Jakobson gives the example of the Russian word *syr* (a food made of fermented pressed curds) which translates roughly into English as *cottage cheese*. In this case, Jakobson claims, the translation is only an adequate *interpretation* of an alien code unit and equivalence is impossible.

Decoding and recoding

The translator, therefore, operates criteria that transcend the purely linguistic, and a process of decoding and recoding takes place. Eugene Nida's model of the translation process illustrates the stages involved:[5]

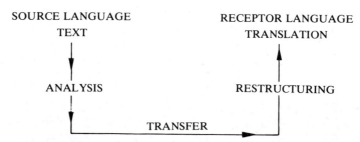

SOURCE LANGUAGE   RECEPTOR LANGUAGE
TEXT   TRANSLATION

ANALYSIS   RESTRUCTURING

TRANSFER

As examples of some of the complexities involved in the interlingual translation of what might seem to be uncontroversial items, consider the question of translating *yes* and *hello* into French, German and Italian. This task would seem, at first glance, to be straightforward, since all are Indo-European languages, closely related lexically and syntactically, and terms of greeting and assent are common to all three. For *yes* standard dictionaries give:

French: *oui, si*
German: *ja*
Italian: *si*

It is immediately obvious that the existence of two terms in French involves a usage that does not exist in the other languages. Further investigation shows that whilst *oui* is the generally used term, *si* is used specifically in cases of contradiction, contention and dissent. The English translator, therefore, must be mindful of this rule when translating the English word that remains the same in all contexts.

When the use of the affirmative in conversational speech is considered, another question arises. *Yes* cannot always be translated into the single words *oui, ja* or *si*, for French, German and Italian all frequently double or 'string' affirmatives in a way that is outside standard English procedures (e.g. *si, si, si*; *ja, ja,* etc.). Hence the Italian or German translation of *yes* by a single word can, at times, appear excessively brusque, whilst the stringing together of affirmatives in English is so hyperbolic that it often creates a comic effect.

With the translation of the word *hello*, the standard English form of friendly greeting when meeting, the problems are multiplied. The dictionaries give:

> French: *ça va?*; *hallo*
> German: *wie geht's*; *hallo*
> Italian: *olà*; *pronto*; *ciao*

Whilst English does not distinguish between the word used when greeting someone face to face and that used when answering the telephone, French, German and Italian all do make that distinction. The Italian *pronto* can only be used as a telephonic greeting, like the German *hallo*. Moreover, French and German use as forms of greeting brief rhetorical questions, whereas the same question in English *How are you?* or *How do you do?* is only used in more formal situations. The Italian *ciao*, by far the most common form of greeting in all sections of Italian society, is used equally on arrival and departure, being a word of greeting linked to a moment of contact between individuals either coming or going and not to the specific context of arrival or initial encounter. So, for example, the translator faced with the task of translating *hello* into French must first extract from the term a core of meaning and the stages of the process, following Nida's diagram, might look like this:

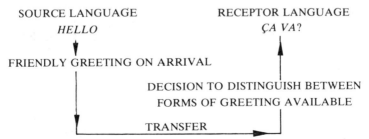

SOURCE LANGUAGE   RECEPTOR LANGUAGE
      HELLO   *ÇA VA?*

FRIENDLY GREETING ON ARRIVAL

                    DECISION TO DISTINGUISH BETWEEN
                    FORMS OF GREETING AVAILABLE

                    TRANSFER

What has happened during the translation process is that the *notion of greeting* has been isolated and the word *hello* has been replaced by a phrase carrying the same notion. Jakobson would describe this as interlingual transposition, while Ludskanov would call it a *semiotic transformation:*

> Semiotic transformations (T_s) are the replacements of the signs encoding a message by signs of another code, preserving (so far as possible in the face of entropy) invariant information with respect to a given system of reference.[6]

In the case of *yes* the invariant information is *affirmation*, whilst in the case of *hello* the invariant is the *notion of greeting*. But at the same time the translator has had to consider other criteria, e.g. the existence of the *oui/si* rule in French, the stylistic function of stringing affirmatives, the *social context* of greeting – whether telephonic or face to face, the class position and status of the speakers and the resultant *weight* of a colloquial greeting in different societies. All such factors are involved in the translation even of the most apparently straightforward word.

The question of semiotic transformation is further extended when considering the translation of a simple noun, such as the English *butter*. Following Saussure, the structural relationship between the signified *(signifié)* or concept of butter and the signifier *(signifiant)* or the sound-image made by the word *butter* constitutes the linguistic sign *butter*.[7] And since language is perceived as a system of interdependent relations, it follows that *butter* operates within English as a noun in a particular structural relationship. But Saussure also distinguished between the syntagmatic (or horizontal) relations that a word has with the words that surround it in a sentence and the associative (or vertical) relations it has with the language structure as a whole. Moreover, within the secondary modelling system there is another type of associative relation and the translator, like the specialist in advertising techniques, must consider both the primary and secondary associative lines. For *butter* in British English carries with it a set of associations of wholesomeness, purity and high status (in comparison to margarine, once perceived only as second-rate butter though now marketed also as practical because it does not set hard under refrigeration).

When translating *butter* into Italian there is a straightforward word-for-word substitution: butter—*burro*. Both *butter* and *burro* describe the product made from milk and marketed as a creamy-coloured slab of edible grease for human consumption. And yet within their separate cultural contexts *butter* and *burro* cannot be considered as signifying the same. In Italy, *burro*, normally light coloured and unsalted, is used primarily for cooking, and carries no associations of high status, whilst in Britain *butter*, most often bright yellow and salted, is used for spreading on bread and less frequently in cooking. Because of the high status of *butter*, the phrase *bread and butter* is the accepted usage even where the product used is actually margarine.[8] So there is a distinction both between the *objects* signified by *butter* and *burro* and between the *function and value* of those objects in their cultural context. The problem of equivalence here involves the utilization and perception of the object in a given context. The *butter—burro* translation, whilst perfectly adequate on one level, also serves as a reminder of the validity of Sapir's statement that each language represents a separate reality.

The word *butter* describes a specifically identifiable product, but in the case of a word with a wider range of SL meanings the problems increase. Nida's diagrammatic sketch of the semantic structure of *spirit* (see p. 20) illustrates a more complex set of semantic relationships.[9]

Where there is such a rich set of semantic relationships as in this case, a word can be used in punning and word-play, a form of humour that operates by confusing or mixing the various meanings (e.g. the jokes about the drunken priest who has been communing too often with the 'holy spirit', etc.). The translator, then, must be concerned with the particular use of *spirit* in the sentence itself, in the sentence in its structural relation to other sentences, and in the overall textual and

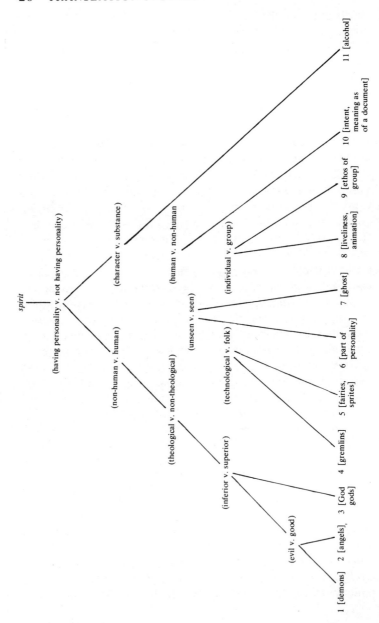

cultural contexts of the sentence. So, for example,

The spirit of the dead child rose from the grave

refers to 7 and not to any other of Nida's categories, whereas

The spirit of the house lived on

could refer to 5 or 7 or, used metaphorically, to 6 or 8 and the meaning can only be determined by the context.

Firth defines meaning as 'a complex of relations of various kinds between the component terms of a context of situation'[10] and cites the example of the English phrase *Say when*, where the words 'mean' what they 'do'. In translating that phrase it is the function that will be taken up and not the words themselves, and the translation process involves a decision to replace and substitute the linguistic elements in the TL. And since the phrase is, as Firth points out, directly linked to English social behavioural patterns, the translator putting the phrase into French or German has to contend with the problem of the non-existence of a similar convention in either TL culture. Likewise, the English translator of the French *Bon appetit* has a similar problem, for again the utterance is situation-bound. As an example of the complexities involved here, let us take a hypothetical dramatic situation in which the phrase *Bon appetit* becomes crucially significant:

> *A family group have been quarreling bitterly, the unity of the family has collapsed, unforgivable things have been said. But the celebratory dinner to which they have all come is about to be served, and the family sit at the table in silence ready to eat. The plates are filled, everyone sits waiting, the father breaks the silence to wish them all 'Bon appetit' and the meal begins.*

Whether the phrase is used mechanically, as part of the daily ritual, whether it is used ironically, sadly or even cruelly is not specified. On a stage, the actor and director would come to a decision about how to interpret the phrase based on their concept of characterization and of the overall meaning and structure of the play. The interpretation would be rendered through voice inflexion. But whatever the interpretation, the significance of the simple utterance cutting into a situation of great tension would remain.

The translator has to take the question of interpretation into account in addition to the problem of selecting a TL phrase which will have a roughly similar meaning. Exact translation is impossible: *Good appetite* in English used outside a structured sentence is meaningless. Nor is there any English phrase in general use that fulfils the same function as the French. There are, however, a series of phrases that might be applicable in certain situations – the colloquial *Dig in* or *Tuck in*, the more formal *Do start*, or even the ritualistically apologetic *I hope you like it,* or *I hope it's alright*. In determining what to use in English, the translator must:

(1) Accept the untranslatability of the SL phrase in the TL on the linguistic level.
(2) Accept the lack of a similar cultural convention in the TL.
(3) Consider the range of TL phrases available, having regard to the presentation of class, status, age, sex of the speaker, his relationship to the listeners and the context of their meeting in the SL.
(4) Consider the significance of the phrase in its particular context – i.e. as a moment of high tension in the dramatic text.
(5) Replace in the TL the invariant core of the SL phrase in its two referential systems (the particular system of the text and the system of culture out of which the text has sprung).

Levý, the great Czech translation scholar, insisted that any contracting or omitting of difficult expressions in translating was immoral. The translator, he believed, had the responsibility of finding a solution to the most daunting of problems, and he declared that the functional view must be adopted with regard not only to meaning but also to style and form. The wealth of studies on Bible translation and the documentation of the way in which individual translators of the Bible attempt to solve their problems through ingenious solutions is a particularly rich source of examples of semiotic transformation.

In translating *Bon appetit* in the scenario given above, the translator was able to extract a set of criteria from the text in order to determine what a suitable TL rendering might be, but clearly in a different context the TL phrase would alter. The emphasis always in translation is on the *reader* or listener, and the translator must tackle the SL text in such a way that the TL version will correspond to the SL version. The nature of that correspondence may vary considerably (see Section 3) but the principle remains constant. Hence Albrecht Neubert's view that Shakespeare's Sonnet 'Shall I compare thee to a summer's day?' cannot be semantically translated into a language where summers are unpleasant is perfectly proper, just as the concept of God the Father cannot be translated into a language where the deity is female. To attempt to impose the value system of the SL culture onto the TL culture is dangerous ground, and the translator should not be tempted by the school that pretends to determine the original *intentions* of an author on the basis of a self-contained text. The translator cannot *be* the author of the SL text, but as the author of the TL text has a clear moral responsibility to the TL readers.

Problems of equivalence

The translation of idioms takes us a stage further in considering the question of meaning and translation, for idioms, like puns, are culture bound. The Italian idiom *menare il can per l'aia* provides a good example of the kind of shift that takes place in the translation process.[11] Translated literally, the sentence

> *Giovanni sta menando il can per l'aia.*

becomes

> *John is leading his dog around the threshing floor.*

The image conjured up by this sentence is somewhat startling and, unless the context referred quite specifically to such a location, the sentence would seem obscure and virtually meaningless. The English idiom that most closely corresponds to the Italian is *to beat about the bush*, also obscure unless used idiomatically, and hence the sentence correctly translated becomes

John is beating about the bush.

Both English and Italian have corresponding idiomatic expressions that render the idea of prevarication, and so in the process of interlingual translation one idiom is substituted for another. That substitution is made not on the basis of the linguistic elements in the phrase, nor on the basis of a corresponding or similar image contained in the phrase, but on the function of the idiom. The SL phrase is replaced by a TL phrase that serves the same purpose in the TL culture, and the process here involves the substitution of SL sign for TL sign. Dagut's remarks about the problems of translating metaphor are interesting when applied also to the problem of tackling idioms:

> Since a metaphor in the SL is, by definition, a new piece of performance, a semantic novelty, it can clearly have no existing 'equivalence' in the TL: what is unique can have no counterpart. Here the translator's bilingual competence – 'le sens', as Mallarmé put it 'de ce qui est dans la langue et de ce qui n'en est pas' – is of help to him only in the negative sense of telling him that any 'equivalence' in this case cannot be 'found' but will have to be 'created'. The crucial question that arises is thus whether a metaphor can, strictly speaking, be translated as *such*, or whether it can only be 'reproduced' in some way.[12]

But Dagut's distinction between 'translation' and 'reproduction', like Catford's distinction between 'literal' and 'free' translation[13] does not take into account the view that sees translation as semiotic transformation. In his definition of translation equivalence, Popovič distinguishes four types:

(1) *Linguistic equivalence,* where there is homogeneity on the linguistic level of both SL and TL texts, i.e. word for word translation.

(2) *Paradigmatic equivalence*, where there is equivalence of 'the elements of a paradigmatic expressive axis', i.e. elements of grammar, which Popovič sees as being a higher category than lexical equivalence.

(3) *Stylistic (translational) equivalence,* where there is 'functional equivalence of elements in both original and translation aiming at an expressive identity with an invariant of identical meaning'.

(4) *Textual (syntagmatic) equivalence*, where there is equivalence of the syntagmatic structuring of a text, i.e. equivalence of form and shape.[14]

The case of the translation of the Italian idiom, therefore, involves the determining of stylistic equivalence which results in the substitution of the SL idiom by an idiom with an equivalent function in the TL.

Translation involves far more than replacement of lexical and grammatical items between languages and, as can be seen in the translation of idioms and metaphors, the process may involve discarding the basic linguistic elements of the SL text so as to achieve Popovič's goal of 'expressive identity' between the SL and TL texts. But once the translator moves away from close linguistic equivalence, the problems of determining the exact nature of the level of equivalence aimed for begin to emerge.

Albrecht Neubert, whose work on translation is unfortunately not available to English readers, distinguishes between the study of translation as a *process* and as a *product*. He states bluntly that: 'the "missing link" between both components of a complete theory of translations appears to be the theory of equivalence relations that can be conceived for both the dynamic and the static model.'[15] The problem of equivalence, a much-used and abused term in Translation Studies, is of central importance, and although Neubert is right when he stresses the need for a theory of equivalence relations, Raymond van den Broeck is also right when he challenges the excessive use of the term in Translation Studies and claims that the precise definition of equivalence in mathematics is a serious obstacle to its use in translation theory.

Eugene Nida distinguishes two types of equivalence, *formal* and *dynamic*, where formal equivalence 'focuses attention on the message itself, in both form and content. In such a translation one is concern with such correspondences as poetry to poetry, sentence to sentence, and concept to concept.' Nida calls this type of translation a 'gloss translation', which aims to allow the reader to understand as much of the SL context as possible. *Dynamic equivalence* is based on the principle of *equivalent effect*, i.e. that the relationship between receiver and message should aim at being the same as that between the original receivers and the SL message. As an example of this type of equivalence, he quotes J.B. Phillips rendering of *Romans* 16:16, where the idea of 'greeting with a holy kiss' is translated as 'give one another a hearty handshake all round'. With this example of what seems to be a piece of inadequate translation in poor taste, the weakness of Nida's loosely defined types can clearly be seen. The principle of *equivalent effect* which has enjoyed great popularity in certain cultures at certain times, involves us in areas of speculation and at times can lead to very dubious conclusions. So E.V. Rieu's deliberate decision to translate Homer into English prose because the significance of the epic form in Ancient Greece could be considered equivalent to the significance of prose in modern Europe, is a case of *dynamic equivalence* applied to the formal properties of a text which shows that Nida's categories can actually be in conflict with each other.

It is an established fact in Translation Studies that if a dozen translators tackle the same poem, they will produce a dozen different versions. And yet somewhere in those dozen versions there will be what Popovič calls the 'invariant core' of the original poem. This invariant core, he claims, is represented

by stable, basic and constant semantic elements in the text,
whose existence can be proved by experimental semantic
condensation. Transformations, or variants, are those changes
which do not modify the core of meaning but influence the
expressive form. In short, the invariant can be defined as that
which exists in common between all existing translations of a
single work. So the invariant is part of a dynamic relationship
and should not be confused with speculative arguments about
the 'nature', the 'spirit' or 'soul' of the text; the 'indefinable
quality' that translators are rarely supposed to be able to
capture.

In trying to solve the problem of translation equivalence,
Neubert postulates that from the point of view of a theory of
texts, translation equivalence must be considered a *semiotic
category*, comprising a *syntactic, semantic* and *pragmatic* component, following Pierce's categories.[16] These components are
arranged in a hierarchical relationship, where semantic
equivalence takes priority over syntactic equivalence, and
pragmatic equivalence conditions and modifies both the other
elements. Equivalence overall results from the relation
between signs themselves, the relationship between signs and
what they stand for, and the relationship between signs, what
they stand for and those who use them. So, for example, the
shock value of Italian or Spanish blasphemous expressions can
only be rendered pragmatically in English by substituting
expressions with sexual overtones to produce a comparable
shock effect, e.g. *porca Madonna — fucking hell.*[17] Similarly,
the interaction between all three components determines the
process of selection in the TL, as for example, in the case of
letter-writing. The norms governing the writing of letters vary
considerably from language to language and from period to
period, even within Europe. Hence a woman writing to a
friend in 1812 would no more have signed her letters *with love*
or *in sisterhood* as a contemporary Englishwoman might, any
more than an Italian would conclude letters without a series of
formal greetings to the recipient of the letter and his relations.
In both these cases, the letter-writing formulae and the

obscenity, the translator decodes and attempts to encode pragmatically.

The question of defining equivalence is being pursued by two lines of development in Translation Studies. The first, rather predictably, lays an emphasis on the special problems of semantics and on the transfer of semantic content from SL to TL. With the second, which explores the question of equivalence of literary texts, the work of the Russian Formalists and the Prague Linguists, together with more recent developments in discourse analysis, have broadened the problem of equivalence in its application to the translation of such texts. James Holmes, for example, feels that the use of the term equivalence is 'perverse', since to ask for sameness is to ask too much, while Durišin argues that the translator of a literary text is not concerned with establishing equivalence of natural language but of artistic procedures. And those procedures cannot be considered in isolation, but must be located within the specific cultural-temporal context within which they are utilized.[18]

Let us take as an example, two advertisements in British Sunday newspaper colour supplements, one for Scotch whisky and one for Martini, where each product is being marketed to cater for a particular taste. The whisky market, older and more traditional than the Martini market, is catered to in advertising by an emphasis on the quality of the product, on the discerning taste of the buyer and on the social status the product will confer. Stress is also laid on the naturalness and high quality of the distilling process, on the purity of Scottish water, and on the length of time the product has matured. The advertisement consists of a written text and a photograph of the product. Martini, on the other hand, is marketed to appeal to a different social group, one that has to be won over to the product which has appeared relatively recently. Accordingly, Martini is marketed for a younger outlook and lays less stress on the question of the quality of the product but much more on the fashionable status that it will confer. The photograph accompanying the brief written text shows 'beautiful people' drinking Martini, members of the international jet set, who inhabit the fantasy world where everyone is supposedly rich and glamourous. These two types of advertisement have become so stereotyped in British culture that they are instantly recognizable and often parodied.

With the advertising of the same two products in an Italian weekly news magazine there is likewise a dual set of images – the one stressing purity, quality, social status; the other stressing glamour, excitement, trendy living and youth. But because Martini is long established and Scotch is a relatively new arrival on the mass market, the images presented with the products are exactly the reverse of the British ones. The same modes, but differently applied, are used in the advertising of these two products in two societies. The products may be the same in both societies, but they have different values. Hence Scotch in the British context may conceivably be defined as the equivalent of Martini in the Italian context, and vice versa, in so far as they are presented through advertising as serving equivalent social functions.

Mukařovský's view that the literary text has both an autonomous and a communicative character has been taken up by Lotman, who argues that a text is *explicit* (it is expressed in definite signs), *limited* (it begins and ends at a given point), and it has *structure* as a result of internal organization. The signs of the text are in a relation of opposition to the signs and structures outside the text. A translator must therefore bear in mind both its autonomous and its communicative aspects and any theory of equivalence should take both elements into account.[19]

Equivalence in translation, then, should not be approached as a search for sameness, since sameness cannot even exist between two TL versions of the same text, let alone between the SL and the TL version. Popovič's four types offer a useful starting point and Neubert's three semiotic categories point the way towards an approach that perceives equivalence as a dialectic between the signs and the structures within and surrounding the SL and TL texts.

Loss and gain

Once the principle is accepted that sameness cannot exist between two languages, it becomes possible to approach the question of *loss and gain* in the translation process. It is again an indication of the low status of translation that so much time should have been spent on discussing what is lost in the transfer of a text from SL to TL whilst ignoring what can also be gained, for the translator can at times enrich or clarify the SL text as a direct result of the translation process. Moreover, what is often seen as 'lost' from the SL context may be replaced in the TL context, as in the case of Wyatt and Surrey's translations of Petrarch (see pp. 56–7; 104–9).

Eugene Nida is a rich source of information about the problems of loss in translation, in particular about the difficulties encountered by the translator when faced with terms or concepts in the SL that do not exist in the TL. He cites the case of Guaica, a language of southern Venezuela, where there is little trouble in finding satisfactory terms for the English *murder, stealing, lying,* etc., but where the terms for *good, bad, ugly* and *beautiful* cover a very different area of meaning. As an example, he points out that Guaica does not follow a dichotomous classification of *good* and *bad*, but a trichotomous one as follows:

(1) *Good* includes desirable food, killing enemies, chewing dope in moderation, putting fire to one's wife to teach her to obey, and stealing from anyone not belonging to the same band.
(2) *Bad* includes rotten fruit, any object with a blemish, murdering a person of the same band, stealing from a member of the extended family and lying to anyone.
(3) *Violating taboo* includes incest, being too close to one's mother-in-law, a married woman's eating tapir before the birth of the first child, and a child's eating rodents.

Nor is it necessary to look so far beyond Europe for examples of this kind of differentiation. The large number of terms in Finnish for variations of snow, in Arabic for aspects of camel behaviour, in English for light and water, in French for types of bread, all present the translator with, on one level, an untranslatable problem. Bible translators have documented the additional difficulties involved in, for example, the concept of the Trinity or the social significance of the parables in certain cultures. In addition to the lexical problems, there are of course languages that do not have tense systems or concepts of time that in any way correspond to Indo-European systems. Whorf's comparison (which may not be reliable, but is cited here as a theoretical example) between a 'temporal language' (English) and a 'timeless language' (Hopi) serves to illustrate this aspect (see Figure 1).[20]

OBJECTIVE FIELD	SPEAKER (SENDER)	HEARER (RECEIVER)	HANDLING OF TOPIC. RUNNING OF THIRD PERSON
SITUATION 1a			ENGLISH...'HE IS RUNNING' HOPI........'WARI' (RUNNING. STATEMENT OF FACT)
SITUATION 1b OBJECTIVE FIELD BLANK DEVOID OF RUNNING			ENGLISH...'HE RAN' HOPI ....'WARI' (RUNNING. STATEMENT OF FACT)
SITUATION 2			ENGLISH...'HE IS RUNNING' HOPI........'WARI' (RUNNING. STATEMENT OF FACT)
SITUATION 3 OBJECTIVE FIELD BLANK			ENGLISH..'HE RAN' HOPI........'ERA WARI' (RUNNING. STATEMENT OF FACT FROM MEMORY)
SITUATION 4 OBJECTIVE FIELD BLANK			ENGLISH...'HE WILL RUN' HOPI........'WARIKNI' (RUNNING. STATEMENT OF EXPECTATION)
SITUATION 5 OBJECTIVE FIELD BLANK			ENGLISH...'HE RUNS'(E.G. ON THE TRACK TEAM) HOPI........ 'WARIKNGWE'(RUNNING. STATEMENT OF LAW)

Figure 1. Whorf's comparison between temporal and timeless languages

Untranslatability

When such difficulties are encountered by the translator, the whole issue of the translatability of the text is raised. Catford distinguishes two types of *untranslatability*, which he terms *linguistic* and *cultural*. On the linguistic level, untranslatability occurs when there is no lexical or syntactical substitute in the TL for an SL item. So, for example, the German *Um wieviel Uhr darf man Sie morgen wecken?* or the Danish *Jeg fandt brevet* are linguistically untranslatable, because both sentences involve structures that do not exist in English. Yet both can be adequately translated into English once the rules of English structure are applied. A translator would unhesitatingly render the two sentences as *What time would you like to be woken tomorrow?* and *I found the letter*, restructuring the German word order and adjusting the position of the postpositive definite article in Danish to conform to English norms.

Catford's category of linguistic untranslatability, which is also proposed by Popovič, is straightforward, but his second category is more problematic. Linguistic untranslatability, he argues, is due to differences in the SL and the TL, whereas cultural untranslatability is due to the absence in the TL culture of a relevant situational feature for the SL text. He quotes the example of the different concepts of the term *bathroom* in an English, Finnish or Japanese context, where both the object and the use made of that object are not at all alike. But Catford also claims that more abstract lexical items such as the English term *home* or *democracy* cannot be described as untranslatable, and argues that the English phrases *I'm going home*, or *He's at home* can 'readily be provided with translation equivalents in most languages' whilst the term *democracy* is international.

Now on one level, Catford is right. The English phrases can be translated into most European languages and *democracy* is an internationally used term. But he fails to take into account two significant factors, and this seems to typify the problem of an overly narrow approach to the question of untranslatability. If *I'm going home* is translated as *Je vais chez moi*, the content meaning of the SL sentence (i.e. self-assertive statement of intention to proceed to place of residence and/or origin) is only loosely reproduced. And if, for example, the phrase is spoken by an American resident temporarily in London, it could either imply a return to the immediate 'home' or a return across the Atlantic, depending on the context in which it is used, a distinction that would have to be spelled out in French. Moreover the English term *home*, like the French *foyer*, has a range of associative meanings that are not translated by the more restricted phrase *chez moi*. *Home*, therefore, would appear to present exactly the same range of problems as the Finnish or Japanese *bathroom*.

With the translation of *democracy*, further complexities arise. Catford feels that the term is largely present in the lexis of many languages and, although it may be relatable to different political situations, the context will guide the reader to select the appropriate situational features. The problem here is that the reader will have a concept of the term based on his or her own cultural context, and will apply that particularized view accordingly. Hence the difference between the adjective *democratic* as it appears in the following three phrases is fundamental to three totally different political concepts:

the American Democratic Party
the German Democratic Republic
the democratic wing of the British Conservative Party.

So although the term is international, its usage in different contexts shows that there is no longer (if indeed there ever was) any common ground from which to select relevant situational features. If culture is perceived as dynamic, then the terminology of social structuring must be dynamic also. Lotman points out that the semiotic study of culture not only considers culture functioning as a system of signs, but emphasizes that 'the *very relation of culture to the sign and to signification* comprises one of its basic typological features.'[21] Catford starts from different premises, and because he does not go far enough in considering the dynamic nature of language and culture, he invalidates his own category of *cultural untranslatability*. In so far as language is the primary modelling system within a culture, cultural untranslatability must be *de facto* implied in any process of translation.

Darbelnet and Vinay, in their useful book *Stylistique comparée du français et de l'anglais* (A Comparative French-English Stylistics),[22] have analysed in detail points of linguistic difference between the two languages, differences that constitute areas where translation is impossible. But once again it is Popovič who has attempted to define untranslatability without making a separation between the linguistic and the cultural. Popovič also distinguishes two types. The first is defined as

> A situation in which the linguistic elements of the original cannot be replaced adequately in structural, linear, functional or semantic terms in consequence of a lack of denotation or connotation.

The second type goes beyond the purely linguistic:

> A situation where the relation of expressing the meaning, i.e. the relation between the creative subject and its linguistic expression in the original does not find an adequate linguistic expression in the translation.

The first type may be seen as parallel to Catford's category of linguistic untranslatability, while into this second type come phrases such as *Bon appetit* or the interesting series of everyday phrases in Danish for expressing thanks. Bredsdorf's Danish grammar for English readers gives elaborate details of the contextual use of such expressions. The explanation of the phrase *Tak for mad*, for example states that 'there is no English equivalent of this expression used to a host or hostess by the guests or members of the household after a meal.'

A slightly more difficult example is the case of the Italian *tamponamento* in the sentence *C'è stato un tamponamento*.

Since English and Italian are sufficiently close to follow a loosely approximate pattern of sentence organization with regard to component parts and word order, the sentence appears fully translatable. The conceptual level is also translatable: an event occurring in time past is being reported in time present. The difficulty concerns the translation of the Italian noun, which emerges in English as a noun phrase. The TL version, allowing for the variance in English and Italian syntax, is

> *There has been/there was a slight accident (involving a vehicle).*

Because of the differences in tense-usage, the TL sentence may take one of two forms depending on the context of the sentence, and because of the length of the noun phrase, this can also be cut down, provided the nature of the accident can be determined outside the sentence by the receiver. But when the significance of *tamponamento* is considered *vis-à-vis* Italian society as a whole, the term cannot be fully understood without some knowledge of Italian driving habits, the frequency with which 'slight accidents' occur and the weighting and relevance of such incidents when they do occur. In short, *tamponamento* is a sign that has a culture-bound or context meaning, which cannot be translated even by an explanatory phrase. The relation between the creative subject and its linguistic expression cannot therefore be adequately replaced in the translation.

Popovič's second type, like Catford's secondary category, illustrates the difficulties of describing and defining the limits of translatability, but whilst Catford starts from within linguistics, Popovič starts from a position that involves a theory of literary communication. Boguslav Lawendowski, in an article in which he attempts to sum up the state of translation studies and semiotics, feels that Catford is 'divorced from reality',[23] while Georges Mounin feels that too much attention has been given to the problem of untranslatability at the expense of solving some of the actual problems that the translator has to deal with.

Mounin acknowledges the great benefits that advances in linguistics have brought to Translation Studies; the development of structural linguistics, the work of Saussure, of Hjelmslev, of the Moscow and Prague Linguistic Circles has been of great value, and the work of Chomsky and the transformational linguists has also had its impact, particularly with regard to the study of semantics. Mounin feels that it is thanks to developments in contemporary linguistics that we can (and must) accept that:

even into words?

(1) Personal experience in its uniqueness is untranslatable.
(2) In theory the base units of any two languages (e.g. phonemes, monemes, etc.) are not always comparable.
(3) Communication is possible when account is taken of the respective situations of speaker and hearer, or author and translator.

In other words, Mounin believes that linguistics demonstrates that translation is a *dialectic process* that can be accomplished with relative success:

> Translation may always start with the clearest situations, the most concrete messages, the most elementary universals. But as it involves the consideration of a language in its entirety, together with its most subjective messages, through an examination of common situations and a multiplication of contacts that need clarifying, then there is no doubt that communication through translation can never be completely finished, which also demonstrates that it is never wholly impossible either.[24]

As has already been suggested, it is clearly the task of the translator to find a solution to even the most daunting of problems. Such solutions may vary enormously; the translator's decision as to what constitutes invariant information with respect to a given system of reference is in itself a creative act. Levý stresses the intuitive element in translating:

> As in all semiotic processes, translation has its *Pragmatic*

dimension as well. Translation theory tends to be normative, to instruct translators on the OPTIMAL solution;
actual translation work, however, is pragmatic; the translator resolves for that one of the possible solutions which
promises a maximum of effect with a minimum of effort.
That is to say, he intuitively resolves for the so-called
MINIMAX STRATEGY.[25]

Science or 'secondary activity'?

The purpose of translation theory, then, is to reach an understanding of the processes undertaken in the act of translation
and, not, as is so commonly misunderstood, to provide a set of
norms for effecting the perfect translation. In the same way,
literary criticism does not seek to provide a set of instructions
for producing the ultimate poem or novel, but rather to understand the internal and external structures operating within and
around a work of art. The pragmatic dimension of translation
cannot be categorized, any more than the 'inspiration' of a text
can be defined and prescribed. Once this point is accepted,
two issues that continue to bedevil Translation Studies can be
satisfactorily resolved; the problem of whether there can be 'a
science of translation' and whether translating is a 'secondary
activity'.

From the above discussion, it would seem quite clear that
any debate about the existence of a science of translation is out
of date: there already exists, with Translation Studies, a
serious discipline investigating the process of translation,
attempting to clarify the question of *equivalence* and to
examine what constitutes *meaning* within that process. But
nowhere is there a theory that pretends to be normative, and
although Lefevere's statement about the goal of the discipline
(see p. 7) suggests that a comprehensive theory might also be
used as a *guideline* for producing translations, this is a long
way from suggesting that the purpose of translation theory is
to be proscriptive.

The myth of translation as a secondary activity with all the associations of lower status implied in that assessment, can be dispelled once the extent of the pragmatic element of translation is accepted, and once the relationship between author/translator/reader is outlined. A diagram of the communicative relationship in the process of translation shows that the translator is both receiver and emitter, the end and the beginning of two separate but linked chains of communication:

Author   —   Text   —   Receiver = Translator   —
Text   —   Receiver

Translation Studies, then, has moved beyond the old distinctions that sought to devalue the study and practice of translation by the use of such terminological distinctions as 'scientific v. creative'. Theory and practice are indissolubly linked, and are not in conflict. Understanding of the processes can only help in the production and, since the product is the result of a complex system of decoding and encoding on the semantic, syntactic and pragmatic levels, it should not be evaluated according to an outdated hierarchical interpretation of what constitutes 'creativity'.

The case for Translation Studies and for translation itself is summed up by Octavio Paz in his short work on translation. All texts, he claims, being part of a literary system descended from and related to other systems, are 'translations of translation of translations':

> Every text is unique and, at the same time, it is the translation of another text. No text is entirely original because language itself, in its essence, is already a translation: firstly, of the non-verbal world and secondly, since every sign and every phrase is the translation of another sign and another phrase. However, this argument can be turned around without losing any of its validity: all texts are original because every translation is distinctive. Every translation, up to a certain point, is an invention and as such it constitutes a unique text.[26]

2 HISTORY OF TRANSLATION THEORY

N O introduction to Translation Studies could be complete without consideration of the discipline in an
historical perspective, but the scope of such an
enterprise is far too vast to be covered adequately in a single
book, let alone in a single chapter. What can be done in the
time and space allowed here is to look at the way in which
certain basic *lines of approach* to translation have emerged at
different periods of European and American culture and to
consider how the role and function of translation has varied.
So, for example, the distinction between *word for word* and
sense for sense translation, established within the Roman
system, has continued to be a point for debate in one way or
another right up to the present, while the relationship between
translation and emergent nationalism can shed light on the
significance of differing concepts of culture. The persecution
of Bible translators during the centuries when scholars were
avidly translating and retranslating Classical Greek and
Roman authors is an important link in the chain of the
development of capitalism and the decline of feudalism. In the
same way, the hermeneutic approach of the great English and
German Romantic translators connects with changing concepts of the role of the individual in the social context. It

cannot be emphasized too strongly that the study of translation, especially in its diachronic aspect, is a vital part of literary and cultural history.

Problems of 'period study'

George Steiner, in *After Babel*,[1] divides the literature on the theory, practice and history of translation into four periods. The first, he claims, extends from the statements of Cicero and Horace on translation up to the publication of Alexander Fraser Tytler's *Essay on the Principles of Translation* in 1791. The central characteristic of this period is that of 'immediate empirical focus', i.e. the statements and theories about translation stem directly from the practical work of translating. Steiner's second period, which runs up to the publication of Larbaud's *Sous l'invocation de Saint Jérome* in 1946 is characterized as a period of theory and hermeneutic enquiry with the development of a vocabulary and methodology of approaching translation. The third period begins with the publication of the first papers on machine translation in the 1940s, and is characterized by the introduction of structural linguistics and communication theory into the study of translation. Steiner's fourth period, coexisting with the third, has its origins in the early 1960s and is characterized by 'a reversion to hermeneutic, almost metaphysical inquiries into translation and interpretation'; in short by a vision of translation that sets the discipline in a wide frame that includes a number of other disciplines:

> Classical philology and comparative literature, lexical statistics and ethnography, the sociology of class-speech, formal rhetoric, poetics, and the study of grammar are combined in an attempt to clarify the act of translation and the process of 'life between languages'.

Steiner's divisions, although interesting and perceptive, nevertheless illustrate the difficulty of studying translation diachronically, for his first period covers a span of some 1700 years while his last two periods cover a mere thirty years. Whilst his comments on recent developments in the discipline are very fair, it is also the case that the characteristic of his first period is equally apparent today in the body of work arising from the observations and polemics of the individual translator. His quadripartite division is, to say the least, highly idiosyncratic, but it does manage to avoid one great pitfall: periodization, or compartmentalization of literary history. It is virtually impossible to divide periods according to dates for, as Lotman points out, human culture is a dynamic system. Attempts to locate stages of cultural development within strict temporal boundaries contradict that dynamism. A splendid example of the kind of difficulties that arise from the 'periodization approach' emerge when we consider the problem of defining the temporal limits of the Renaissance. There is a large body of literature that attempts to decide whether Petrarch and Chaucer were medieval or Renaissance writers, whether Rabelais was a medieval mind *post hoc*, or whether Dante was a Renaissance mind two centuries too soon. An examination of translation in those terms would not be very helpful at all.

Yet undoubtably there are certain concepts of translation that prevail at different times, which can be documented. T.R. Steiner[2] analyses English translation theory between the cut-off dates of 1650–1800, starting with Sir John Denham and ending with William Cowper, and examines the prevailing eighteenth-century concept of the translator as painter or imitator. André Lefevere[3] has compiled a collection of statements and documents on translation that traces the establishment of a German tradition of translation, starting with Luther and moving on via Gottsched and Goethe to the Schlegels and Schleiermacher and ultimately to Rosenzweig. A less systematic approach, but one which is still tied to a particular time frame, may be found in F.O. Matthiesson's analysis of four major English translators of the sixteenth century (Hoby, North, Florio and Philemon Holland),[4] whilst the methodology employed by Timothy Webb in his study of

Shelley as translator[5] involves a careful analysis of the work of an individual translator in relation to the rest of his opus and to contemporary concepts of the role and status of translation.

Studies of this kind, then, that are not bound to rigid notions of period, but seek to investigate changing concepts of translation systematically, having regard to the system of signs that constitutes a given culture, are of great value to the student of Translation Studies. This is indeed a rich field for future research. All too often, however, studies of past translators and translations have focused more on the question of *influence*; on the effect of the TL product in a given cultural context, rather than on the processes involved in the creation of that product and on the theory behind the creation. So, for example, in spite of a number of critical statements about the significance of translation in the development of the Roman literary canon, there has yet to be a systematic study of Roman translation theory in English. The claims summed up by Matthiesson when he declared that 'a study of Elizabethan translations is a study of the means by which the Renaissance came to England' are not backed by any scientific investigation of the same.

In trying to establish certain lines of approach to translation, across a time period that extends from Cicero to the present, it seems best to proceed by following a loosely chronological structure, but without making any attempt to set up clear-cut divisions. Hence, instead of trying to talk in what must inevitably be very general terms about a specifically 'Renaissance' or 'Classical' concept of translation, I have tried to follow *lines of approach* that may or may not be easily locatable in a temporal context. So the *word for word* v. *sense for sense* lines can be seen emerging again and again with different degrees of emphasis in accordance with differing concepts of language and communication. The purpose of a chapter such as this must be to raise questions rather than answer them, and to reveal areas in which further research might proceed rather than to pretend to be a definitive history.

The Romans

Eric Jacobsen[6] claims rather sweepingly that translation is a Roman invention, and although this may be considered as a piece of critical hyperbole, it does serve as a starting point from which to focus attention on the role and status of translation for the Romans. The views of both Cicero and Horace on translation were to have great influence on successive generations of translators, and both discuss translation within the wider context of the two main functions of the poet: the universal human duty of acquiring and disseminating wisdom and the special art of making and shaping a poem.

The significance of translation in Roman literature has often been used to accuse the Romans of being unable to create imaginative literature in their own right, at least until the first century BC. Stress has been laid on the creative imagination of the Greeks as opposed to the more practical Roman mind, and the Roman exaltation of their Greek models has been seen as evidence of their lack of originality. But the implied value judgement in such a generalization is quite wrong. The Romans perceived themselves as a continuation of their Greek models and Roman literary critics discussed Greek texts without seeing the language of those texts as being in any way an inhibiting factor. The Roman literary system sets up a hierarchy of texts and authors that overrides linguistic boundaries and that system in turn reflects the Roman ideal of the hierarchical yet caring central state based on the true law of Reason. Cicero points out that mind dominates the body as a king rules over his subjects or a father controls his children, but warns that where Reason dominates as a master ruling his slaves, 'it keeps them down and crushes them'.[7] With translation, the ideal SL text is there to be imitated and not to be crushed by the too rigid application of Reason. Cicero nicely expresses this distinction: 'If I render word for word, the result will sound uncouth, and if compelled by necessity I alter anything in the order or wording, I shall seem to have departed from the function of a translator.'[8]

Both Horace and Cicero, in their remarks on translation,

make an important distinction between *word for word* translation and *sense for sense* (or *figure for figure*) translation. The underlying principle of enriching their native language and literature through translation leads to a stress on the aesthetic criteria of the TL product rather than on more rigid notions of 'fidelity'. Horace, in his *Art of Poetry*, warns against overcautious imitation of the source model:

> A theme that is familiar can be made your own property so long as you do not waste your time on a hackneyed treatment; nor should you try to render your original word for word like a slavish translator, or in imitating another writer plunge yourself into difficulties from which shame, or the rules you have laid down for yourself, prevent you from extricating yourself.[9]

Since the process of the enrichment of the literary system is an integral part of the Roman concept of translation, it is not surprising to find a concern with the question of language enrichment also. So prevalent was the habit of borrowing or coining words, that Horace, whilst advising the would-be writer to avoid the pitfalls that beset 'the slavish translator', also advised the sparing use of new words. He compared the process of the addition of new words and the decline of other words to the changing of the leaves in spring and autumn, seeing this process of enrichment through translation as both natural and desirable, *provided* the writer exercised moderation. The art of the translator, for Horace and Cicero, then, consisted in judicious interpretation of the SL text so as to produce a TL version based on the principle *non verbum de verbo, sed sensum exprimere de sensu* (of expressing not word for word, but sense for sense), and his responsibility was to the TL readers.

But there is also an additional dimension to the Roman concept of enrichment through translation, i.e. the pre-eminence of Greek as the language of culture and the ability of educated Romans to read texts in the SL. When these factors are taken into account, then the position both of translator and reader alters. The Roman reader was generally able to consider the translation as a metatext in relation to the original. The translated text was read *through* the source text, in contrast to the way in which a monolingual reader can only approach the SL text through the TL version. For Roman translators, the task of transferring a text from language to language could be perceived as an exercise in comparative stylistics, since they were freed from the exigencies of having to 'make known' either the form or the content *per se*, and consequently did not need to subordinate themselves to the frame of the original. The good translator, therefore, presupposed the reader's acquaintance with the SL text and was bound by that knowledge, for any assessment of his skill as translator would be based on the creative use he was able to make of his model. Longinus, in his *Essay On the Sublime*,[10] cites 'imitation and emulation of the great historians and poets of the past' as one of the paths towards the sublime and translation is one aspect of imitation in the Roman concept of literary production.

Roman translation may therefore be perceived as unique in that it arises from a vision of literary production that follows an established canon of excellence across linguistic boundaries. Moreover, it should not be forgotten that with the extension of the Roman Empire, bilingualism and trilingualism became increasingly commonplace, and the gulf between oral and literary Latin widened. The apparent licence of Roman translators, much quoted in the seventeenth and eighteenth centuries, must therefore be seen in the context of the overall system in which that approach to translation was applied.

Bible translation

With the spread of Christianity, translation came to acquire another role, that of disseminating the word of God. A religion as text-based as Christianity presented the translator with a mission that encompassed both aesthetic and evangelistic criteria. The history of Bible translation is accordingly a history of western culture in microcosm. Translations of the New Testament were made very early, and St Jerome's famous contentious version that was to have such influence on succeeding generations of translators was commissioned by Pope Damasus in 384 AD. Following Cicero, St Jerome declared he had translated sense for sense rather than word for word, but the problem of the fine line between what constituted stylistic licence and what constituted heretical interpretation was to remain a major stumbling block for centuries.

Bible translation remained a key issue well into the seventeenth century, and the problems intensified with the growth of concepts of national cultures and with the coming of the Reformation. Translation came to be used as a weapon in both dogmatic and political conflicts as nation states began to emerge and the centralization of the church started to weaken, evidenced in linguistic terms by the decline of Latin as a universal language.[11]

The first translation of the complete Bible into English was the Wycliffite Bible produced between 1380 and 1384, which marked the start of a great flowering of English Bible transla-tions linked to changing attitudes to the role of the written text in the church, that formed part of the developing Reforma-tion. John Wycliffe (c. 1330–84), the noted Oxford theologian, put forward the theory of 'dominion by grace' according to which man was immediately responsible to God and God's law (by which Wycliffe intended not canon law but the guidance of the Bible). Since Wycliffe's theory meant that the Bible was applicable to all human life it followed that each man should be granted access to that crucial text in a language that he could understand, i.e. in the vernacular. Wycliffe's views, which attracted a circle of followers, were attacked as heretical and he and his group were denounced as 'Lollards', but the work he began continued to flourish after his death and his disciple John Purvey revised the first edition some time before 1408 (the first dated manuscript).

The second Wycliffite Bible contains a general Prologue, composed between 1395–6 and the fifteenth chapter of the Prologue describes the four stages of the translation process:

(1) a collaborative effort of collecting old Bibles and glosses and establishing an authentic Latin source text;
(2) a comparison of the versions;
(3) counselling 'with old grammarians and old divines' about hard words and complex meanings; and
(4) translating as clearly as possible the 'sentence' (i.e. meaning), with the translation corrected by a group of collaborators.

Since the political function of the translation was to make the complete text of the Bible accessible, this led to a definite stance on priorities by the translator: Purvey's Preface states clearly that the translator shall translate 'after the sentence' (meaning) and not only after the words, 'so that the sentence be as open [plain] or opener, in English as in Latin and go not far from the letter.' What is aimed at is an intelligible, idiomatic version: a text that could be utilized by the layman. The extent of its importance may be measured by the fact that the bulk of the 150 copies of Purvey's revised Bible were written even after the prohibition, on pain of excommunication, of translations circulated without the approval of diocesan or provincial councils in July 1408. Knyghton the Chronicler's lament that 'the Gospel pearl is cast abroad, and trodden under feet of swine' was certainly contradicted by the widespread interest in the Wycliffite versions.

In the sixteenth century the history of Bible translation acquired new dimensions with the advent of printing. After the Wycliffite versions, the next great English translation was William Tyndale's (1494–1536) New Testament printed in 1525. Tyndale's proclaimed intention in translating was also to offer as clear a version as possible to the layman, and by the time he was burned at the stake in 1536 he had translated the New Testament from the Greek and parts of the Old Testament from the Hebrew.

The sixteenth century saw the translation of the Bible into a large number of European languages, in both Protestant and Roman Catholic versions. In 1482, the Hebrew Pentateuch had been printed at Bologna and the complete Hebrew Bible appeared in 1488, whilst Erasmus, the Dutch Humanist, published the first Greek New Testament in Basle in 1516. This version was to serve as the basis for Martin Luther's 1522 German version. Translations of the New Testament appeared in Danish in 1529 and again in 1550, in Swedish in 1526–41, and the Czech Bible appeared between 1579–93. Translations and revised versions of existing translations continued to appear in English, Dutch, German and French. Erasmus perhaps summed up the evangelizing spirit of Bible translating when he declared

> I would desire that all women should reade the gospell and
> Paules episteles and I wold to God they were translated in
> to the tonges of all men so that they might not only be read
> and knowne of the scotes and yrishmen But also of the
> Turkes and the Sarracenes. . . . I wold to God the plowman
> wold singe a texte of the scripture at his plow-beme. And
> that the wever at his lowme with this wold drive away the
> tediousnes of tyme. I wold the wayfaringeman with this
> pastyme wold expelle the weriness of his iorney. And to be
> shorte I wold that all the communication of the christen
> shuld be of the scripture for in a manner such are we oure
> selves as our daylye tales are.[12]

William Tyndale, echoing Erasmus, attacked the hypocrisy of church authorities who forbade the laypeople to read the Bible in their native tongue for the good of their souls, but nevertheless accepted the use of the vernacular for 'histories and fables of love and wantoness and of ribaudry as filthy as heart can think, to corrupt the minds of youth.'

The history of Bible translation in the sixteenth century is intimately tied up with the rise of Protestantism in Europe. The public burning of Tyndale's New Testament in 1526 was followed in quick succession by the appearance of Coverdale's

Bible (1535), the Great Bible (1539) and the Geneva Bible in 1560. Coverdale's Bible was also banned but the tide of Bible translation could not be stemmed, and each successive version drew on the work of previous translators, borrowing, amending, revising and correcting.

It would not perhaps be too gross a generalization to suggest that the aims of the sixteenth-century Bible translators may be collocated in three categories:

(1) To clarify errors arising from previous versions, due to inadequate SL manuscripts or to linguistic incompetence.
(2) To produce an accessible and aesthetically satisfying vernacular style.
(3) To clarify points of dogma and reduce the extent to which the scriptures were interpreted and re-presented to the laypeople as a metatext.

In his *Circular Letter on Translation* of 1530 Martin Luther lays such emphasis on the significance of (2) that he uses the verbs *übersetzen* (to translate) and *verdeutschen* (to Germanize) almost indiscriminately. And Luther also stresses the importance of the relationship between style and meaning: 'Grammar is necessary for declension, conjugation and construction of sentences, but in speech the meaning and subject matter must be considered, not the grammar, for the grammar shall not rule over the meaning.'[13]

The Renaissance Bible translators perceived both fluidity and intelligibility in the TL text as important criteria, but were equally concerned with the transmission of a literally accurate message. In an age when the choice of a pronoun could mean the difference between life or condemnation to death as a heretic, precision was of central importance. Yet because Bible translation was an integral part of the upward shift in the status of the vernacular, the question of style was also vital. Luther advised the would-be translator to use a vernacular proverb or expression if it fitted in with the New Testament, in other words to add to the wealth of imagery in the SL text by drawing on the vernacular tradition too. And since the Bible is in itself a text that each individual reader must reinterpret in the reading, each successive translation attempts to allay doubts in the wording and offer readers a text in which they may put their trust. In the Preface to the King James Bible of 1611, entitled *The Translators to the Reader*, the question is asked 'is the kingdom of God words or syllables?' The task of the translator went beyond the linguistic, and became evangelistic in its own right, for the (often anonymous) translator of the Bible in the sixteenth century was a radical leader in the struggle to further man's spiritual progress. The collaborative aspect of Bible translation represented yet another significant aspect of that struggle.

Education and the vernacular

The educative role of translation of the Scriptures was well-established long before the fifteenth and sixteenth centuries, and the early vernacular glosses inserted in Latin manuscripts have provided valuable information concerning the development of a number of European languages. With regard to English, for example, the Lindisfarne Gospels (copied out *c.* 700 AD), had a literal rendering of the Latin original inserted between the lines in the tenth century in Northumbrian dialect. These glosses subordinated notions of stylistic excellence to the word-for-word method, but may still be fairly described as translations, since they involved a process of interlingual transfer. However, the system of glossing was only one aspect of translation in the centuries that saw the emergence of distinct European languages in a written form. In the ninth century King Alfred (reign 871–99), who had translated (or caused to be translated) a number of Latin texts, declared that the purpose of translating was to help the English people to recover from the devastation of the Danish invasions that had laid waste the old monastic centres of learning and had demoralized and divided the kingdom. In his Preface to his translation of the *Cura Pastoralis* (a handbook for parish priests) Alfred urges a revival of learning through greater accessibility of texts as a direct result of translations into the vernacular, and at the same time he asserts the claims of English as a literary language in its own right. Discussing the way in which the Romans translated texts for their own purposes, as did 'all other Christian nations', Alfred states that 'I think it better, if you agree, that we also translate some of the books that all men should know into the language that we can all understand.'[14] In translating the *Cura Pastoralis*, Alfred claims to have followed the teachings of his bishop and priests and to have rendered the text *hwilum word be worde, hwilum andgiet of andgiete* (sometimes word by word, sometimes sense by sense), an interesting point in that it implies that the function of the finished product was the determining factor in the translation process rather than any established canon of procedure. Translation is perceived as having a moral and didactic purpose with a clear political role to play, far removed from its purely instrumental role in the study of rhetoric that coexisted at the same time.

The concept of translation as a writing exercise and as a means of improving oratorical style was an important component in the medieval educational system based on the study of the Seven Liberal Arts. This system, as passed down from such Roman theoreticians as Quintilian (first century AD) whose *Institutio Oratoria* was a seminal text, established two areas of study, the *Trivium* (grammar, rhetoric and dialectic) and the *Quadrivium* (arithmetic, geometry, music and astronomy), with the Trivium as the basis for philosophical knowledge.[15]

Quintilian stresses the usefulness of paraphrasing a given text as a means of assisting the student both to analyse the structures of a text and to experiment in turn with forms of embellishment or abridgement. He prescribes paraphrasing as a set of exercises that move through two distinct stages: the initial straightforward closeness of a first paraphrase and the more complex second stage when the writer adds more of his own style. Together with these exercises, Quintilian advocates translation, and indeed the two activities are not clearly distinguished since both are employed to the same end: that of improving the science of oratory. Quintilian recommends translating from Greek into Latin as a variation on paraphrasing original Latin texts in order to extend and develop the student's imaginative powers.

Quintilian's advocacy of translation as a stylistic exercise involved, of course, the translation of Greek originals into Latin, and Latin remained the language of the educational system throughout Europe for centuries. But the emergence of vernacular literatures from the tenth century onwards led to another shift in the role of translation. Alfred had extolled the importance of translation as a means of spreading understanding, and for him translation involved the creation of a *vernacular* SL text. As emerging literatures with little or no written tradition of their own to draw upon developed across Europe, works produced in other cultural contexts were translated, adapted and absorbed on a vast scale. Translation acquired an additional dimension, as writers used their abilities to translate as a means of increasing the status of their own vernacular. Thus the Roman model of enrichment through translation developed in a new form.

In his useful article on vulgarization and translation, Gianfranco Folena suggests that medieval translation might be described either as *vertical*, by which he intends translation into the vernacular from a SL that has a special prestige or value (e.g. Latin), or as *horizontal*, where both SL and TL have a similar value (e.g. Provençal into Italian, Norman-French into English).[16] Folena's distinction, however, is not new: Roger Bacon (*c.* 1214–92) was well aware of the differences between translating from ancient languages into Latin and translating contemporary texts into the vernacular, as was Dante (1265–1321), and both talk about translation in relation to the moral and aesthetic criteria of works of art and scholarship. Bacon, for example, discusses the problem of *loss* in translation and the counter-issue, that of coinage, as Horace had done centuries earlier. Meanwhile Dante focuses more on the importance of *accessibility* through translation. But both agree that translation involves much more than an exercise in comparative stylistics.

The distinction between *horizontal* and *vertical* translation is helpful in that it shows how translation could be linked to two coexistent but different literary systems. However, there are many different strands in the development of literary translation up to the early fifteenth century and Folena's distinction only sheds light on one small area. And whilst the *vertical* approach splits into two distinct types, the interlinear gloss, or word-for-word technique, as opposed to the Ciceronian sense-for-sense method, elaborated by Quintilian's concept of paraphrase, the *horizontal* approach involves complex questions of *imitatio* and borrowing. The high status of *imitatio* in the medieval canon meant that originality of material was not greatly prized and an author's skill consisted in the reworking of established themes and ideas. The point at which a writer considered himself to be a translator of another text, as opposed to the use he might make of translated material plagiarized from other texts, is rarely clear. Within the opus of a single writer, such as Chaucer (*c*. 1340–1400) there is a range of texts that include acknowledged translations, free adaptations, conscious borrowings, reworkings and close correspondences. And although theoreticians such as Dante or John of Trevisa (1326–1412) raise the question of *accuracy* in translation, that notion of accuracy is dependent on the translator's ability to read and understand the original and does not rest on the translator's subordination to that SL text. Translation, whether vertical or horizontal, is viewed as a skill, inextricably bound up with modes of reading and interpreting the original text, which is proper source material for the writer to draw upon as he thinks fit.

Early theorists

Following the invention of printing techniques in the fifteenth century, the role of translation underwent significant changes, not least due to the great increase in the volume of translations undertaken. At the same time, serious attempts to formulate a theory of translation were also made. The function of translation, together with the function of learning itself changed. For as the great voyages of discovery opened up a world outside Europe, increasingly sophisticated clocks and instruments for measuring time and space developed and these, together with the theory of the Copernican universe, affected concepts of culture and society and radically altered perspectives.

One of the first writers to formulate a theory of translation was the French humanist Etienne Dolet (1509–46) who was tried and executed for heresy after 'mistranslating' one of Plato's dialogues in such a way as to imply disbelief in immortality. In 1540 Dolet published a short outline of translation principles, entitled *La manière de bien traduire d'une langue en aultre* (How to Translate Well from one Language into Another) and established five principles for the translator:

(1) The translator must fully understand the sense and meaning of the original author, although he is at liberty to clarify obscurities.
(2) The translator should have a perfect knowledge of both SL and TL.
(3) The translator should avoid word-for-word renderings.
(4) The translator should use forms of speech in common use.
(5) The translator should choose and order words appropriately to produce the correct tone.

Dolet's principles, ranked as they are in a precise order, stress the importance of *understanding* the SL text as a primary requisite. The translator is far more than a competent linguist, and translation involves both a scholarly and sensitive appraisal of the SL text and an awareness of the place the translation is intended to occupy in the TL system.

Dolet's views were reiterated by George Chapman (1559–1634), the great translator of Homer. In his dedication of the *Seven Books* (1598) Chapman declares that

The work of a skilfull and worthy translator is to observe the sentences, figures and formes of speech proposed in his author, his true sence and height, and to adorne them with figures and formes of oration fitted to the originall in the same tongue to which they are translated: and these things I would gladlie have made the questions of whatsoever my labours have deserved.[17]

He repeats his theory more fully in the *Epistle to the Reader* of his translation of *The Iliad*. In the *Epistle* Chapman states that a translator must:

(1) avoid word for word renderings;
(2) attempt to reach the 'spirit' of the original;
(3) avoid overloose translations, by basing the translation on a sound scholarly investigation of other versions and glosses.

The Platonic doctrine of the divine inspiration of poetry clearly had repercussions for the translator, in that it was deemed possible for the 'spirit' or 'tone' of the original to be recreated in another cultural context. The translator, therefore, is seeking to bring about a 'transmigration' of the original text, which he approaches on both a technical and metaphysical level, as a skilled equal with duties and responsibilities both to the original author and the audience.

The Renaissance

Edmond Cary, discussing Dolet in his study of the great French translators, stresses the importance of translation in the sixteenth century:

The translation battle raged throughout Dolet's age. The Reformation, after all, was primarily a dispute between translators. Translation became an affair of State and a matter of Religion. The Sorbonne and the king were equally concerned with it. Poets and prose writers debated the matter, Joachim du Bellay's *Défense et Illustration de la*

Langue française is organized around problems relating to translation.[18]

In such an atmosphere, where a translator could be executed as a result of a particular rendering of a sentence or phrase in text, it is hardly surprising that battle lines were drawn with vehemence. The quality of aggressive assertiveness that can be discerned in Chapman's *Epistle* or Dolet's pamphlet can be seen through the work and statements of a number of translators of the time. One major characteristic of the period (reflected also in the number of translations of the Bible that updated the language of preceding versions without necessarily making major interpretative changes) is an affirmation of the present through the use of contemporary idiom and style. Matthiesson's study of Elizabethan translators gives a number of examples of the way in which the affirmation of the individual in his own time manifests itself. He notes, for example, the frequent replacement of indirect discourse by direct discourse in North's translation of Plutarch (1579), a device that adds immediacy and vitality to the text, and quotes examples of North's use of lively contemporary idiom. So in North's version it is said of Pompey that 'he did lay all the irons in the fire he could, to bring it to pass that he might be chosen dictator' (V, p. 30–1) and of Anthony that he decided Caesar's body should 'be honourably buried and not in hugger mugger' (VI, p. 200).

In poetry, the adjustments made to the SL text by such major translators as Wyatt (1503–42) and Surrey (*c.* 1517–47) have led critics to describe their translations at times as 'adaptations', but such a distinction is misleading. An investigation of Wyatt's translations of Petrarch, for example, shows a faithfulness not to individual words or sentence structures but to a notion of the meaning of the poem in its relationship to its readers. In other words, the poem is perceived as an artefact of a particular cultural system, and the only faithful translation can be to give it a similar function in the target cultural system. For example, Wyatt takes Petrarch's famous sonnet on the events of 1348 with the death of Cardinal Giovanni Colonna and of Laura that begins

> Rotta è l'alta colonna e'l verde lauro
> Che facean ombra al mio stanco pensero;   (CCLXIX)
> (Broken is the tall column (Colonna) and the green laurel
>   tree (Laura)
> That used to shade my tired thought)

and turns it into:

> The pillaɼ pearished is whearto I lent;
> The strongest staye of myne unquyet mynde:
>
> (CCXXXVI)

It is clear that he is using the translation process to do something other than render Petrarch's words line for line or recapture the elegiac quality of the original. Wyatt's translation stresses the 'I', and stresses also the strength and support of what is lost. Whether the theory that would see this sonnet as written in commemoration of the fall of Cromwell in 1540 is proven or not, it remains clear that the translator has opted for a voice that will have immediate impact on contemporary readers as being of their own time.

The updating of texts through translation by means either of additions, omissions or conscious alterations can be very clearly seen in the work of Philemon Holland (1552–1637) the 'translator general'. In translating Livy he declared that his aim was to ensure that Livy should 'deliver his mind in English, if not so eloquently by many degrees, yet as truly as in Latine', and claimed that he used not 'any affected phrase, but . . . a meane and popular style'. It is his attempt at such a style that led to such alterations as the use of contemporary terminology for certain key Roman terms, so, for example *patres et plebs* becomes *Lords* or *Nobles and Commons*; *comitium* can be *common hall, High court, Parliament; praetor* becomes *Lord Chiefe Justice* or *Lord Governour of the City*. At other times, in his attempt to clarify obscure passages and references he inserts explanatory phrases or sentences and above all his confident nationalism shows through. In the

Preface to the Reader of his translation of Pliny, Holland attacks those critics who protest at the vulgarization of Latin classics and comments that they 'think not so honourably of their native country and mother tongue as they ought', claiming that if they did they would be eager to 'triumph over the Romans in subduing their literature under the dent of the English pen' in revenge for the Roman conquest of Britain effected in earlier times by the sword.

Translation in Renaissance Europe came to play a role of central importance. As George Steiner puts it:

> At a time of explosive innovation, and amid a real threat of surfeit and disorder, translation absorbed, shaped, oriented the necessary raw material. It was, in a full sense of the term, the *matière première* of the imagination. Moreover, it established a logic of relation between past and present, and between different tongues and traditions which were splitting apart under stress of nationalism and religious conflict.[19]

Translation was by no means a secondary activity, but a primary one, exerting a shaping force on the intellectual life of the age, and at times the figure of the translator appears almost as a revolutionary activist rather than the servant of an original author or text.

The seventeenth century

By the mid-seventeenth century the effects of the Counter-Reformation, the conflict between absolute monarchy and the developing Parliamentary system, and the widening of the gap between traditional Christian Humanism and science had all led to radical changes in the theory of literature and hence to the role of translation. Descartes' (1596–1650) attempts to formulate a method of inductive reasoning were mirrored in the preoccupation of literary critics to formulate rules of aesthetic production. In their attempt to find models, writers turned to ancient masters, seeing in *imitation* a means of instruction. Translation of the classics increased considerably in France between 1625 and 1660, the great age of French classicism and of the flowering of French theatre based on the Aristotelian unities. French writers and theorists were in turn enthusiastically translated into English.

The emphasis on rules and models in Augustan England did not mean, however, that art was perceived as a merely imitative skill. Art was the ordering in a harmonious and elegant manner of Nature, the inborn ability that transcended definition and yet prescribed the finished form. Sir John Denham (1615–69), whose theory of translation, as expressed in his poem 'To Sir Richard Fanshawe upon his Translation of Pastor Fido' (1648) and in his Preface to his translation of *The Destruction of Troy* (1656) (see below) covers both the formal aspect (Art) and the spirit (Nature) of the work, but warns against applying the principle of literal translation to the translation of poetry:

> for it is not his business alone to translate Language into Language, but Poesie into Poesie; and Poesie is of so subtile a spirit, that in pouring out of one Language into another, it will all evaporate; and if a new spirit be not added in the transfusion, there will remain nothing but a *Caput mortuum*.[20]

Denham argues for a concept of translation that sees translator and original writer as equals but operating in clearly differentiated social and temporal contexts. He sees it as the translator's duty to his source text to extract what he perceives as the essential core of the work and to reproduce or recreate the work in the target language.

Abraham Cowley (1618–67) goes a stage further, and in his 'Preface' to his *Pindarique Odes* (1656) he boldly asserts that he has 'taken, left out and added what I please' in his translations, aiming not so much at letting the reader know precisely what the original author said as 'what was his way and manner of speaking'. Cowley makes a case for his manner of translating, dismissing those critics who will choose (like Dryden) to term his form of translation 'imitation', and T.R. Steiner notes that Cowley's preface was taken as the manifesto of the 'libertine translators of the latter seventeenth century'.

John Dryden (1631–1700), in his important Preface to Ovid's Epistles (1680), tackled the problems of translations by formulating three basic types:

(1) *metaphrase*, or turning an author word by word, and line by line, from one language into another;

(2) *paraphrase,* or translation with latitude, the Ciceronian 'sense-for-sense' view of translation;

(3) *imitation,* where the translator can abandon the text of the original as he sees fit.

Of these types Dryden chooses the second as the more balanced path, provided the translator fulfils certain criteria: to translate poetry, he argues, the translator must be a poet, must be a master of both languages, and must understand both the characteristics and 'spirit' of the original author, besides conforming to the aesthetic canons of his own age. He uses the metaphor of the translator/portrait painter, that was to reappear so frequently in the eighteenth century, maintaining that the painter has the duty of making his portrait resemble the original.

In his *Dedication of the Aeneis* (1697) Dryden claims to have followed his prescribed path of moderation and to have steered 'betwixt the two extremes of paraphrase and literal translation', but following French models he has updated the language of his original text: 'I have endeavoured to make Virgil speak such English as he would himself have spoken, if he had been born in England, and in this present age.' As an example of Dryden's version of Virgil, consider the opening lines of Dido's speech describing her thoughts about Aeneas in the decorous language of a contemporary heroine:

> My dearest Anna! What new dreams affright
> My labouring soul! What visions of the night
> Disturb my quiet, and distract my breast
> With strange ideas of our Trojan guest.[21]

Dryden's views on translation were followed fairly closely by Alexander Pope (1688–1744), who advocates the same middle ground as Dryden, with stress on close reading of the original to note the details of style and manner whilst endeavouring to keep alive the 'fire' of the poem.

The eighteenth century

Underlying Dryden's and Pope's concept of translation is another element, beyond the problem of the debate between overfaithfulness and looseness: the whole question of the moral duty of the translator to his contemporary reader. The impulse to clarify and make plain the essential *spirit* of a text led to large-scale rewritings of earlier texts to fit them to contemporary standards of language and taste. Hence the famous re-structuring of Shakespearian texts, and the translations/reworkings of Racine. Dr Johnson (1709–84), in his *Life of Pope* (1779–80), discussing the question of additions to a text through translation, comments that if elegance is gained, surely it is desirable, provided nothing is taken away, and goes on to state that 'the purpose of a writer is to be read', claiming that Pope wrote for his own time and his own nation. The right of the individual to be addressed in his own terms, on his own ground is an important element in eighteenth-century translation and is linked to changing concepts of 'originality'.

To exemplify the particular approach Pope brought to his version of Homer, compare the following passage to Chapman's version of an episode from Book 22 of *The Iliad*. Pope's Andromache suffers and despairs, whilst Chapman's Andromache comes across as a warrior in her own right. Chapman's use of direct verbs gives a dramatic quality to the scene, whilst Pope's Latinate structures emphasize the agony of expectation leading up to the moment when the horror is plain to see. And even that horror is quite differently presented – Pope's 'god-like Hector' contrasts with Chapman's longer description of the hero's degradation:[22]

She spoke; and furious, with distracted Pace,
Fears in her Heart and Anguish in her Face,
Flies through the Dome, (the maids her steps pursue)
And mounts the walls, and sends around her view.
Too soon her Eyes the killing Object found,
The god-like Hector dragg'd along the ground.
A sudden Darkness shades her swimming Eyes:
She faints, she falls; her Breath, her colour flies. (Pope)

        Thus fury-like she went,
Two women, as she will'd, at hand; and made her quick
ascent
Up to the tower and press of men, her spirit in
uproar. Round
She cast her greedy eye, and saw her Hector slain, and
bound
T'Achilles chariot, manlessly dragg'd to the Grecian fleet,
Black night strook through her, under her trance took away
her feet. (Chapman)

The eighteenth-century concept of the translator as painter or imitator with a moral duty both to his original subject and to his receiver was widespread, but underwent a series of significant changes as the search to codify and describe the processes of literary creation altered. Goethe (1749–1832) argued that every literature must pass through three phases of translation, although as the phases are recurrent all may be found taking place within the same language system at the same time. The first epoch 'acquaints us with foreign countries on our own terms', and Goethe cites Luther's German Bible as an example of this tendency. The second mode is that of appropriation through substitution and reproduction, where the translator absorbs the sense of a foreign work but reproduces it in his own terms, and here Goethe cites Wieland and the French tradition of translating (a tradition much disparaged by German theorists). The third mode, which he considers the highest, is one which aims for perfect identity between the SL text and the TL text, and the achieving of this mode must be through the creation of a new 'manner' which fuses the uniqueness of the original with a new form and structure. Goethe cites the work of Voss, who translated Homer, as an example of a translator who had achieved this prized third level. Goethe is arguing for both a new concept of 'originality' in translation, together with a vision of universal deep structures that the translator should strive to meet. The problem with such an approach is that it is moving dangerously close to a theory of untranslatability.

Towards the end of the eighteenth century, in 1791, Alexander Fraser Tytler published a volume entitled *The Principles of Translation*, the first systematic study in English of the translation processes.[23] Tytler set up three basic principles:

(1) The translation should give a complete transcript of the idea of the original work.
(2) The style and manner of writing should be of the same character with that of the original.
(3) The translation should have all the ease of the original composition.

Tytler reacts against Dryden's influence, maintaining that the concept of 'paraphrase' had led to exaggeratedly loose translations, although he agrees that part of the translator's duty is to clarify obscurities in the original, even where this entails omission or addition. He uses the standard eighteenth-century comparison of the translator/painter, but with a difference, arguing that the translator cannot use the same colours as the original, but is nevertheless required to give his picture 'the same force and effect'. The translator must strive to 'adopt the very soul of his author, which must speak through his own organs'.

Translation theory from Dryden to Tytler, then, is concerned with the problem of recreating an essential spirit, soul or nature of the work of art. But the earlier confident dichotomy between the formal structure and the inherent soul becomes less easily determinable as writers gradually turned their attention towards a discussion of theories of Imagination, away from the former emphasis on the artist's moral role, and from what Coleridge described as 'painful copying' that 'would produce masks only, not forms breathing life'.[24]

Romanticism

In his great standard work on European Romanticism, *Le romantisme dans la littérature européenne* (1948), Paul van Tieghem describes the movement as 'une crise de la conscience européenne'.[25] Although the crisis is intimated much earlier in the eighteenth century, the extent of the reaction against rationalism and formal harmony (the Neo-classical ideals), began to be clear in the last decade of the century, together with the ever-widening shock waves that followed the French Revolution of 1789. With the rejection of rationalism came a stress on the vitalist function of the imagination, on the individual poet's world-vision as both a metaphysical and a revolutionary ideal. With the affirmation of individualism came the notion of the freedom of the creative force, making the poet into a quasi-mystical creator, whose function was to produce the poetry that would create anew the universe, as Shelley argued in *The Defence of Poesy* (1820).

Goethe's distinctions between types of translation and stages in a hierarchy of aesthetic evaluation is indicative of a change in attitude to translation resulting from a revaluation of the role of poetry and creativity. In England, Coleridge (1772–1834) in his *Biographia Literaria* (1817) outlined his theory of the distinction between Fancy and Imagination, asserting that Imagination is the supreme creative and organic power, as opposed to the lifeless mechanism of Fancy. This theory has affinities with the theory of the opposition of mechanical and organic form outlined by the German theorist and translator, August Wilhelm Schlegel (1767–1845) in his *Vorlesungen über dramatische Kunst und Literatur* (1809), translated into English in 1813. Both the English and German theories raise the question of how to define translation – as a creative or as a mechanical enterprise. In the Romantic debate on the nature of translation the ambiguous attitude of a number of major writers and translators can be seen. A.W. Schlegel, asserting that all acts of speaking and writing are acts of translation because the nature of communication is to decode and interpret messages received, also insisted that the form of the original should be retained (for example, he retained Dante's *terza rima* in his own translations). Meanwhile, Friedrich Schlegel (1772–1829) conceived of translation as a category of thought rather than as an activity connected only with language or literature.

The ideal of a great shaping spirit that transcends the everyday world and recreates the universe led to re-evaluation of the poet's role in time, and to an emphasis on the rediscovery of great individuals of the past who shared a common sense of creativity. The idea of writers at all times being involved in a process of repeating what Blake called 'the Divine Body in Every Man' resulted in a vast number of translations, such as the Schlegel-Tieck translations of Shakespeare (1797–1833), Schlegel's version and Cary's version of the *Divina Commedia* (1805–14) and the large intertraffic of translations of critical works and of contemporary writings across the European languages. Indeed, so many texts were translated at this time that were to have a seminal effect on the TL (e.g. German authors into English and vice versa, Scott and Byron into French and Italian, etc.) that critics have found it difficult to distinguish between influence study and translation study proper. Stress on the impact of the translation in the target culture in fact resulted in a shift of interest away from the actual processes of translation. Moreover, two conflicting tendencies can be determined in the early nineteenth century. One exalts translation as a category of thought, with the translator seen as a creative genius in his own right, in touch with the genius of his original and enriching the literature and language into which he is translating. The other sees translation in terms of the more mechanical function of 'making known' a text or author.

The pre-eminence of the Imagination as opposed to the Fancy leads implicitly to the assumption that translation must be inspired by the higher creative force if it is to become more than an activity of the everyday world with the loss of the original shaping spirit. But this raises another problem also: the problem of *meaning*. If poetry is perceived as a separate entity from language, how can it be translated unless it is assumed that the translator is able to read between the words of the original and hence reproduce the text-behind-the-text; what Mallarmé would later elaborate as the text of silence and spaces?

In his study of Shelley and translation Timothy Webb shows how the ambiguousness of the role of the translator is reflected in the poet's own writings. Quoting from Shelley's works and from Medwin, his biographer, Webb demonstrates that Shelley saw translation as an activity with a lower status, as a 'way of filling in the gaps between inspirations', and points out that Shelley appears to shift from translating works admired for their ideas to translating works admired for their literary graces. This shift is significant, for in a sense it follows Goethe's hierarchy of translating and it shows the problem that translation posed in the establishment of a Romantic aesthetic. Most important of all, with the shift of emphasis away from the formal processes of translation, the notion of untranslatability would lead on to the exaggerated emphasis on technical accuracy and resulting pedantry of later nineteenth-century translating. The assumption that meaning lies below and between language created an impasse for the translator. Only two ways led out of the predicament:

(1) the use of literal translation, concentrating on the immediate language of the message; or
(2) the use of an artificial language somewhere in between the SL text where the special feeling of the original may be conveyed through strangeness.

Post-Romanticism

Friedrich Schleiermacher (1768–1834) proposed the creation of a separate sub-language for use in translated literature only, while Dante Gabriel Rossetti (1828–82) proclaimed the translator's subservience to the forms and language of the original. Both these proposals represent attempts to cope with the difficulties described so vividly by Shelley in *The Defence of Poesy* when he warned that:

> It were as wise to cast a violet into a crucible that you might discover the formal principle of its colour and odour, as to seek to transfuse from one language into another the creations of a poet. The plant must spring again from its seed, or it will bear no flower – and this is the burthen of the curse of Babel.[26]

Schleiermacher's theory of a separate translation language was shared by a number of nineteenth-century English translators, such as F.W. Newman, Carlyle and William Morris. Newman declared that the translator should retain every peculiarity of the original wherever possible, 'with the greater care the more foreign it may be',[27] while an explanation of the function of peculiarity can be found in G.A. Simcox's review of Morris' translation of *The Story of the Volsungs and Niblungs* (1870) when he declared that the 'quaint archaic English of the translation with just the right outlandish flavour' did much to 'disguise the inequalities and incompletenesses of the original'.[28]

William Morris (1834–96) translated a large number of texts, including Norse sagas, Homer's *Odyssey*, Vergil's *Aeneid*, Old French romances, etc., and received considerable critical aclaim. Oscar Wilde wrote of Morris' *Odyssey* that it was 'a true work of art, a rendering not merely of language into language, but of poetry into poetry'. He noted, however, that the 'new spirit added in the transfusion' was more Norse than Greek, and this opinion is a good illustration of the expectations the nineteenth-century reader might have of a translation. Morris' translations are deliberately, consciously archaic, full of such peculiarities of language that they are difficult to read and often obscure. No concessions are made to the reader, who is expected to deal with the work on its own terms, meeting head-on, through the strangeness of the TL, the foreignness of the society that originally produced the text. The awkwardness of Morris' style can be seen in the following passage, taken from Book VI of the *Aeneid*:

> What God, O Palinure, did snatch thee so away
> From us thy friends and drown thee dead amidst the watery way?
> Speak out! for Seer Apollo, found no guileful prophet erst,
> By this one answer in my soul a lying hope hath nursed;
> Who sang of thee safe from the deep and gaining field and fold
> Of fair Ausonia: suchwise he his plighted word doth hold![29]

The Victorians

The need to convey the remoteness of the original in time and place is a recurrent concern of Victorian translators. Thomas Carlyle (1795–1881), who used elaborate Germanic structures in his translations from the German, praised the profusion of German translations claiming that the Germans studied other nations 'in spirit which deserves to be oftener imitated' in order to be able to participate in 'whatever worth or beauty' another nation had produced.[30] Dante Gabriel Rossetti (1828–82) in his Preface to his translations from Early Italian Poets (1861) declared similarly that 'The only true motive for putting poetry into a fresh language must be to endow a fresh nation, as far as possible, with one more possession of beauty',[31] noting, however, that the originals were often obscure and imperfect.

What emerges from the Schleiermacher-Carlyle-Pre-Raphaelite concept of translation, therefore, is an interesting paradox. On the one hand there is an immense respect, verging on adulation, for the original, but that respect is based on the individual writer's sureness of its worth. In other words, the translator invites the intellectual, cultivated reader to share what he deems to be an enriching experience, either on moral or aesthetic grounds. Moreover, the original text is perceived as *property*, as an item of beauty to be added to a collection, with no concessions to the taste or expectations of contemporary life. On the other hand, by producing consciously archaic translations designed to be read by a minority, the translators implicitly reject the ideal of universal literacy. The intellectual reader represented a very small minority in the increasingly diffuse reading public that expanded throughout the century, and hence the foundations were laid for the notion of translation as a minority interest.

Matthew Arnold (1822–68) in his first lecture *On Translating Homer* advises the lay reader to put his trust in scholars, for they alone can say whether the translation produces more or less the same effect as the original and gives the following advice to the would-be translator:

> Let not the translator, then, trust to his notions of what the ancient Greeks would have thought of him; he will lose himself in the vague. Let him not trust to what the ordinary English reader thinks of him; he will be taking the blind for his guide. Let him not trust to his own judgement of his own work; he may be misled by individual caprices. Let him ask how his work affects those who both know Greek and can appreciate poetry.[32]

The translator must focus on the SL text primarily, according to Arnold, and must serve that text with complete commitment. The TL reader must be brought to the SL text through the means of the translation, a position that is the opposite of the one expressed by Erasmus when discussing the need for accessibility of the SL text. And with the hardening of nationalistic lines and the growth of pride in a national culture, French, English or German translators, for example, no longer saw translation as a prime means of enriching their own culture. The élitist concept of culture and education embodied in this attitude was, ironically, to assist in the devaluation of translation. For if translation were perceived as an instrument, as a means of bringing the TL reader to the SL text *in the original*, then clearly excellence of style and the translator's own ability to write were of less importance. Henry Wadsworth Longfellow (1807–81) added another dimension to the question of the role of the translator, one which restricted the translator's function even more than Arnold's dictum. Discussing his translation of Dante's *Divina Commedia*, and defending his decision to translate into blank verse, Longfellow declared:

> The only merit my book has is that it is exactly what Dante says, and not what the translator imagines he might have said if he had been an Englishman. In other words, while making it rhythmic, I have endeavoured to make it also as literal as a prose translation. . . . In translating Dante, something must be relinquished. Shall it be the beautiful rhyme that blossoms all along the line like a honeysuckle on the hedge? It must be, in order to retain something more precious than rhyme, namely, fidelity, truth, – the life of the hedge itself. . . . The business of a translator is to report what the author says, not to explain what he means; that is the work of the commentator. What an author says and how he says it, that is the problem of the translator.[33]

Longfellow's extraordinary views on translation take the literalist position to extremes. For him, the rhyme is mere trimming, the floral border on the hedge, and is distinct from the life or truth of the poem itself. The translator is relegated to the position of a technician, neither poet nor commentator, with a clearly defined but severely limited task.

In complete contrast to Longfellow's view, Edward Fitzgerald (1809–63), who is best known for his version of *The Rubaiyat of Omar Khayyam* (1858), declared that a text must live at all costs 'with a transfusion of one's own worst Life if one can't retain the Original's better'. It was Fitzgerald who made the famous remark that it were better to have a live sparrow than a stuffed eagle. In other words, far from attempting to lead the TL reader to the SL original, Fitzgerald's work seeks to bring a version of the SL text into the TL culture as *a living entity*, though his somewhat extreme views on the lowliness of the SL text, quoted in the Introduction (p. 3), indicate a patronizing attitude that demonstrates another form of élitism. The Romantic individualist line led on, in translators like Fitzgerald, to what Eugene Nida describes as a 'spirit of exclusivism', where the translator appears as a skilful merchant offering exotic wares to the discerning few.

The main currents of translation typology in the great age of industrial capitalism and colonial expansion up to the First World War can loosely be classified as follows:

(1) Translation as a scholar's activity, where the preeminence of the SL text is assumed *de facto* over any TL version.

(2) Translation as a means of encouraging the intelligent reader to return to the SL original.

(3) Translation as a means of helping the TL reader become the equal of what Schleiermacher called the better reader of the original, through a deliberately contrived foreignness in the TL text.

(4) Translation as a means whereby the individual translator who sees himself like Aladdin in the enchanted vaults (Rossetti's imaginative image) offers his own pragmatic choice to the TL reader.

(5) Translation as a means through which the translator seeks to upgrade the status of the SL text because it is perceived as being on a lower cultural level.

From these five categories, it can be seen that types (1) and (2) would tend to produce very literal, perhaps pedantic translations, accessible to a learned minority, whilst types (4) and (5) could lead to much freer translations that might alter the SL text completely in the individual translator's eclectic process of treating the original. The third category, perhaps the most interesting and typical of all, would tend to produce translations full of archaisms of form and language, and it is this method that was so strongly attacked by Arnold when he coined the verb *to newmanize*, after F.W. Newman, a leading exponent of this type of translation.

Archaizing

J.M. Cohen feels that the theory of Victorian translation was founded on 'a fundamental error' (i.e. that of conveying remoteness of time and place through the use of a mock antique language),[34] and the pedantry and archaizing of many translators can only have contributed to setting translation apart from other literary activities and to its steady decline in status. Fitzgerald's method of translation, in which the SL text was perceived as the rough clay from which the TL product was moulded, certainly enjoyed great popular success, but it is significant that a debate arose around whether to define his work as a translation or as something else (adaptation, version, etc.) which is indicative of the existence of a general view of what a translation ought to be. But although archaizing has gone out of fashion, it is important to remember that there were sound theoretical principles for its adoption by translators. George Steiner raises important issues when he discusses the practice, with particular reference to Emile Littré's theory and his *L'Enfer mis en vieux langage François* (1879) and to Rudolf Borchardt and his *Dante Deutsch*:

> The proposition 'the foreign poet would have produced such and such a text had he been writing in my language' is a projective fabrication. It underwrites the autonomy, more exactly, the 'meta-autonomy' of the translation. But it does much more: it introduces an alternate existence, a 'might have been' or 'is yet to come' into the substance and historical condition of one's own language, literature and legacy of sensibility.[35]

The archaizing principle, then, in an age of social change on an unprecedented scale, can be compared to an attempt to 'colonize' the past. As Borchardt put it, declaring that the translation should restore something to the original: 'The circle of the historical exchange of forms between nations closes in that Germany returns to the foreign object what it has learnt from it and freely improved upon.'[36] The distance between this version of translation and the vision of Cicero and Horace, also the products of an expanding state, could hardly be greater.

The twentieth century

It is always a problem, in attempting to compress a vast amount of material into a short space, to decide on a cut-off point at which to bring the discussion to a close. George Steiner ends his second period of translation history in 1946, with Valery Larbaud's fascinating but unsystematic work *Sous l'invocation de Saint Jerome*, whilst Cohen's study of English translator's and translations tails off rather lamely with occasional references to some of the practical translation work of Robert Graves and C. Day Lewis, and so brings the reader sketchily into the 1950s. Much of the discussion in English on translation in theory and practice in the first half of the twentieth century notes the continuation of many of the Victorian concepts of translation – literalness, archaizing, pedantry and the production of a text of second-rate literary merit for an élite minority. But it then returns continually to the problem of evaluation *without a solid theoretical base from which to begin such an investigation*. The increased isolationism of British and American intellectual life, combined with the anti-theoretical developments in literary criticism did not help to further the scientific examination of translation in English. Indeed, it is hard to believe, when considering some of the studies in English, that they were written in the same age that saw the rise of Czech Structuralism and the New Critics, the development of communication theory, the application of linguistics to the study of translation: in short, to the establishment of the bases from which recent work in translation theory has been able to proceed.

The progress of the development of Translation Studies has been discussed in the earlier parts of this book, and the steady growth of valuable works on translation in English since the late 1950s has been noted. But it would be wrong to see the first half of the twentieth century as the Waste Land of English translation theory, with here and there the fortresses of great individual translators approaching the issues pragmatically. The work of Ezra Pound is of immense importance in the history of translation, and Pound's skill as a translator was matched by his perceptiveness as critic and theorist. Hilaire Belloc's Taylorian lecture *On Translation*, given in 1931, is a brief but highly intelligent and systematic approach to the practical problems of translating and to the whole question of the status of the translated text. James McFarlane's article 'Modes of Translation' (1953) raised the level of the discussion of translation in English, and has been described as 'the first publication in the West to deal with translation and translations from a modern, interdisciplinary view and to set out a program of research for scholars concerned with them as an object of study'.[37]

From this brief outline, it can clearly be seen that different concepts of translation prevail at different times, and that the function and role of the translator has radically altered. The explanation of such shifts is the province of cultural history, but the effect of changing concepts of translation on the process of translating itself will occupy researchers for a long time to come. George Steiner, taking a rather idiosyncratic view of translation history, feels that although there is a profusion of pragmatic accounts by individuals the range of theoretic ideas remains small:

> List Saint Jerome, Luther, Dryden, Hölderlin, Novalis, Schleiermacher, Nietzsche, Ezra Pound, Valéry, Mac-Kenna, Franz Rosenzweig, Walter Benjamin, Quine – and you have very nearly the sum total of those who have said anything fundamental or new about translation.[38]

But Steiner's description of the translator as a shadowy presence, like Larbaud's description of the translator as a beggar
at the church door, is essentially a post-Romantic view, and
has far more to do with notions of hierarchy in the chain of
communication between author, text, reader and translator
than with any intrinsic aspect of the process of translation
itself. Timothy Webb's study of Shelley as translator, for
example, documents the growing split between types of literary activity, and shows how a hierarchy could exist within the
work of a single author in early nineteenth-century England.
For the attitudes towards translation and the concepts of
translation that prevail, belong to the age that produces them,
and to the socio-economic factors that shape and determine
that age. Maria Corti has shown how through the nineteenth
century, due to the wider distribution of the printed book, the
author could no longer see his public so clearly, either because
it was potentially so vast or because it cut across classes and
social groups. For the translator this problem of impaired
vision was all the more acute.[39]

The history of Translation Studies should therefore be seen
as an essential field of study for the contemporary theorist, but
should not be approached from a narrowly fixed position.
Gadda's definition of system can most aptly be applied to the
diachronics of Translation Studies and serves as an illustration
of the size and complexity of the work that has barely been
begun:

> We therefore think of every system as an infinite entwining,
> an inextricable knot or mesh of relations: the summit can
> be seen from many altitudes; and every system is referable
> to infinite coordinated axes: it presents itself in infinite
> ways.[40]

3 SPECIFIC PROBLEMS OF LITERARY TRANSLATION

I N the Introduction to this book I affirmed the need for a close relationship between the theory and the practice of translation. The translator who makes no attempt to understand the *how* behind the translation process is like the driver of a Rolls who has no idea what makes the car move. Likewise, the mechanic who spends a lifetime taking engines apart but never goes out for a drive in the country is a fitting image for the dry academician who examines the *how* at the expense of *what is*. In this third section I propose, therefore, to approach the question of the translation of literary works through close analysis of examples, not so much to evaluate the products but rather to show how specific problems of translation can emerge from the individual translators' selection of criteria.

Structures

Anne Cluysenaar, in her book on literary stylistics, makes some important points about translation. The translator, she believes, should not work with general precepts when determining what to preserve or parallel from the SL text, but should work with an eye 'on each individual structure, whether it be prose or verse', since 'each structure will lay stress on certain linguistic features or levels and not on others'. She goes on to analyse C. Day Lewis' translation of Valéry's poem, *Les pas* and comes to the conclusion that the translation does not work because the translator 'was working without an adequate theory of literary translation'. What Day Lewis has done, she feels, is to have ignored the relation of parts to each other and to the whole and that his translation is, in short, 'a case of perceptual "bad form" '. The remedy for such inadequacies is also proposed: what is needed, says Cluysenaar, 'is a description of the dominant structure of every individual work to be translated.'[1]

Cluysenaar's assertive statements about literary translation derive plainly from a structuralist approach to literary texts that conceives of a text as a set of related systems, operating within a set of other systems. As Robert Scholes puts it:

> Every literary unit from the individual sentence to the whole order of words can be seen in relation to the concept of system. In particular, we can look at individual works, literary genres, and the whole of literature as related systems, and at literature as a system within the larger system of human culture.[2]

The failure of many translators to understand that a literary text is made up of a complex set of systems existing in a dialectical relationship with other sets outside its boundaries has often led them to focus on particular aspects of a text at the expense of others. Studying the average reader, Lotman determines four essential positions of the addressee:

(1) Where the reader focuses on the content as matter, i.e. picks out the prose argument or poetic paraphrase.
(2) Where the reader grasps the complexity of the structure of a work and the way in which the various levels interact.
(3) Where the reader deliberately extrapolates one level of the work for a specific purpose.
(4) Where the reader discovers elements not basic to the

genesis of the text and uses the text for his own purposes.[3]

Clearly, for the purposes of translation, position (1) would be completely inadequate (although many translators of novels in particular have focused on content at the expense of the formal structuring of the text), position (2) would seem an ideal starting point, whilst positions (3) and (4) might be tenable in certain circumstances. The translator is, after all, first a reader and then a writer and in the process of reading he or she must take a position. So, for example, Ben Belitt's translation of Neruda's *Fulgor y muerte de Joaquín Murieta* contains a statement in the Preface about the rights of the reader to expect 'an American sound not present in the inflection of Neruda', and one of the results of the translation is that the political line of the play is completely changed. By stressing the 'action', the 'cowboys and Indians myth' element, the dialectic of the play is destroyed, and hence Belitt's translation could be described as an extreme example of Lotman's third reader position.[4]

The fourth position, in which the reader discovers elements in the text that have evolved since its genesis, is almost unavoidable when the text belongs to a cultural system distanced in time and space. The twentieth-century reader's dislike of the Patient Griselda motif is an example of just such a shift in perception, whilst the disappearance of the epic poem in western European literatures has inevitably led to a change in reading such works. On the semantic level alone, as the meaning of words alters, so the reader/translator will be unable to avoid finding himself in Lotman's fourth position without detailed etymological research. So when Gloucester, in King Lear, Act III sc.vii, bound, tormented and about to have his eyes gouged out, attacks Regan with the phrase 'Naughty lady', it ought to be clear that there has been considerable shift in the weight of the adjective, now used to admonish children or to describe some slightly comic (often sexual) peccadillo.

Much time and ink has been wasted attempting to

differentiate between *translations, versions, adaptations* and the establishment of a hierarchy of 'correctness' between these categories. Yet the differentiation between them derives from a concept of the reader as the passive receiver of the text in which its Truth is enshrined. In other words, if the text is perceived as an object that should only produce a single invariant reading, any 'deviation' on the part of the reader/ translator will be judged as a transgression. Such a judgement might be made regarding scientific documents, for example, where facts are set out and presented in unqualifiedly objective terms for the reader of SL and TL text alike, but with literary texts the position is different. One of the greatest advances in twentieth-century literary study has been the re-evaluation of the reader. So Barthes sees the place of the literary work as that of making the reader not so much a consumer as a *producer* of the text,[5] while Julia Kristeva sees the reader as realizing the expansion of the work's process of semiosis.[6] The reader, then, *translates* or *decodes* the text according to a different set of systems and the idea of the one 'correct' reading is dissolved. At the same time, Kristeva's notion of *intertextuality*, that sees all texts linked to all other texts because no text can ever be completely free of those texts that precede and surround it, is also profoundly significant for the student of translation. As Paz suggests (see p. 38) all texts are translations of translations of translations and the lines cannot be drawn to separate Reader from Translator.

Quite clearly, the idea of the reader as translator and the enormous freedom this vision bestows must be handled responsibly. The reader/translator who does not acknowledge the dialectical materialist basis of Brecht's plays or who misses the irony in Shakespeare's sonnets or who ignores the way in which the doctrine of the transubstantiation is used as a masking device for the production of Vittorini's anti-Fascist statement in *Conversazioni in Sicilia* is upsetting the balance of power by treating the original as his own property. And all these elements can be missed if the reading does not take into full account the overall structuring of the work and its relation to the time and place of its production. Maria Corti sums up the role of the reader in terms that could equally be seen as advice to the translator:

> Every era produces its own type of signedness, which is made to manifest in social and literary models. As soon as these models are consumed and reality seems to vanish, new signs become needed to recapture reality, and this allows us to assign an information-value to the dynamic structures of literature. So seen, literature is both the condition and the place of artistic communication between senders and addressees, or public. The messages travel along its paths, in time, slowly or rapidly; some of the messages venture into encounters that undo an entire line of communication; but after great effort a new line will be born. This last fact is the most significant; it requires apprenticeship and dedication on the part of those who would understand it, because the hypersign function of great literary works transforms the grammar of our view of the world.[7]

The translator, then, first reads/translates in the SL and then, through a further process of decoding, translates the text into the TL language. In this he is not doing less than the reader of the SL text alone, he is actually doing more, for the SL text is being approached through more than one set of systems. It is therefore quite foolish to argue that the task of the translator is to translate but not to interpret, as if the two were separate exercises. The interlingual translation is bound to reflect the translator's own creative interpretation of the SL text. Moreover, the degree to which the translator reproduces the form, metre, rhythm, tone, register, etc. of the SL text, will be as much determined by the TL system as by the SL system and will also depend on the function of the translation. If, as in the case of the Loeb Classics Library, the translation is intended as a line by line crib on the facing page to the SL text, then this factor will be a major criterion. If, on the other hand, the SL text is being reproduced for readers with no knowledge either of the language or the socio-literary conventions of the SL system, then the translation will be constructed in terms other than those employed in the bilingual version. It has already been pointed out in Section 2 that criteria governing modes of translation have varied considerably throughout the ages and there is certainly no single proscriptive model for translators to follow.

Poetry and translation

Within the field of literary translation, more time has been devoted to investigating the problems of translating poetry than any other literary mode. Many of the studies purporting to investigate these problems are either evaluations of different translations of a single work or personal statements by individual translators on how they have set about solving problems.[8] Rarely do studies of poetry and translation try to discuss methodological problems from a non-empirical position, and yet it is precisely that type of study that is most valuable and most needed.

In his book on the various methods employed by English translators of Catullus' *Poem 64*,[9] André Lefevere catalogues seven different strategies:

(1) *Phonemic translation*, which attempts to reproduce the SL sound in the TL while at the same time producing an acceptable paraphrase of the sense. Lefevere comes to the conclusion that although this works moderately well in the translation of onomatopoeia, the overall result is clumsy and often devoid of sense altogether.

(2) *Literal translation,* where the emphasis on word-for-word translation distorts the sense and the syntax of the original.

(3) *Metrical translation*, where the dominant criterion is the reproduction of the SL metre. Lefevere concludes that, like literal translation, this method concentrates on one aspect of the SL text at the expense of the text as a whole.

(4) *Poetry into prose*. Here Lefevere concludes that distor-

tion of the sense, communicative value and syntax of the SL text results from this method, although not to the same extent as with the literal or metrical types of translation.

(5) *Rhymed translation*, where the translator 'enters into a double bondage' of metre and rhyme. Lefevere's conclusions here are particularly harsh, since he feels that the end product is merely a 'caricature' of Catullus.

(6) *Blank verse translation*. Again the restrictions imposed on the translator by the choice of structure are emphasized, although the greater accuracy and higher degree of literalness obtained are also noted.

(7) *Interpretation*. Under this heading, Lefevere discusses what he calls *versions* where the substance of the SL text is retained but the form is changed, and *imitations* where the translator produces a poem of his own which has 'only title and point of departure, if those, in common with the source text'.

What emerges from Lefevere's study is a revindication of the points made by Anne Cluysenaar, for the deficiencies of the methods he examines are due to an overemphasis of one or more elements of the poem at the expense of the whole. In other words, in establishing a set of methodological criteria to follow, the translator has focused on some elements at the expense of others and from this failure to consider the poem as an organic structure comes a translation that is demonstrably unbalanced. However, Lefevere's use of the term *version* is rather misleading, for it would seem to imply a distinction between this and *translation*, taking as the basis for the argument a split between form and substance. Yet, as Popovič points out,[10] 'the translator has the right to differ organically, to be independent', provided that independence is pursued for the sake of the original in order to reproduce it as a living work.

In his article, 'The Poet as Translator', discussing Pound's *Homage to Sextus Propertius*, J.P. Sullivan recalls asking Pound why he had used the phrase 'Oetian gods' instead of

'Oetian God' (i.e. Hercules) in Section I of the poem. Pound had replied simply that it would 'bitch the movement of the verse'. And earlier, in the same article, Sullivan quotes Pound defending himself against the savage attacks on his work in the following terms:

> No, I have not done a translation of Propertius. That fool in Chicago took the *Homage* for a translation despite the mention of Wordsworth and the parodied line from Yeats. (As if, had one wanted to pretend to more Latin than one knew, it wouldn't have been perfectly easy to correct one's divergencies from a Bohn crib. Price 5/-.)[11]

For Pound, the distinction between his translations and his *Homage* was clear, but for those critics schooled in nineteenth-century notions of the excellence of literalness, the distinction was irrelevant. Pound had very precise ideas about the responsibility of the translator, but his frame of reference would have been far closer to Popovič's than to Professor W.G. Hale's.[12] Pound defined his *Homage* as something other than a translation; his purpose in writing the poem, he claimed, was to bring a dead man to life. It was, in short, a kind of literary resurrection.

The greatest problem when translating a text from a period remote in time is not only that the poet and his contemporaries are dead, but *the significance of the poem in its context* is dead too. Sometimes, as with the pastoral, for example, the genre is dead and no amount of fidelity to the original form, shape or tone will help the rebirth of a new line of communication, to use Maria Corti's terms, *unless the TL system is taken into account equally.* With the classics, this first means overcoming the problem of translating along a vertical axis, where the SL text is seen as being of a higher status than the TL text. Unless the translation is intended as a crib, it also means accepting Popovič's theory of the inevitability of shifts of expression in the translation process.[13]

As an example of the way in which different concepts of translation can be applied to the translation of a classical author, let us take three versions of Catullus *Poem 13*.

An Invitation to Dinner

Cenabis bene, mi Fabulle, apud me
paucis, si tibi di favent, diebus,
si tecum attuleris bonam atque magnam
cenam, non sine candida puella
et vino et sale et omnibus cachinnis.
haec, si, inquam, attuleris, venuste noster,
cenabis bene; nam tui Catulli
plenus sacculus est aranearum.
sed contra accipies meros amores
seu quid suavius elegantiusve est:
nam unguentum dabo, quod meae puellae
donarunt Veneres Cupidinesque,
quod tu cum olfacies, deos rogabis,
totum ut te faciant, Fabulle, nasum.

(Catullus, 13)

(1)   Now, please the gods, Fabullus, you
Shall dine here well in a day or two;
But bring a good big dinner, mind,
Likewise a pretty girl, and wine
And wit and jokes of every kind.
Bring these, I say, good man, and dine
Right well: for your Catullus' purse
Is full – but only cobwebs bears.
But you with love itself I'll dose,
Or what still sweeter, finer is,
An essence to my lady given
By all the Loves and Venuses;
Once sniff it, you'll petition heaven
To make you nose and only nose.

(Sir William Marris, 1924)

(2)   say Fabullus
you'll get a swell dinner at my house
a couple three days from now (if your luck holds out)

all you gotta do is bring the dinner
    and make it good and be sure there's plenty
Oh yes don't forget a girl (I like blondes)
and a bottle of wine maybe
    and any good jokes and stories you've heard
just do that like I tell you ol' pal ol' pal
you'll get a swell dinner
    ?
    what,
      about,
        ME?
well;
    well here take a look in my wallet,
      yeah those're cobwebs
but here,
    I'll give you something too
      I CAN'T GIVE YOU ANYTHING BUT
      LOVE BABY
no?
well here's something nicer and a little more cherce
                    maybe
I got perfume see
it was a gift to HER
    straight from VENUS and CUPID LTD.
when you get a whiff of that you'll pray the gods
to make you (yes you will, Fabullus)
    ALL
      NOSE
             (Frank O. Copley, 1957)

(3)   Inviting a friend to supper

    To night, grave sir, both my poore house, and I
    Doe equally desire your companie:
    Not that we thinke us worthy such a ghest,
    But that your worth will dignifie our feast,
    With those that come; whose grace may make that
                    seeme

Something, which, else, could hope for no esteeme.
It is the faire acceptance, Sir, creates
The entertaynment perfect: not the cates.
Yet shall you have, to rectifie your palate,
An olive, capers, or some better sallade
Ushring the mutton; with a short-leg'd hen,
If we can get her, full of egs, and then,
Limons, and wine for sauce: to these, a coney
Is not to be despair'd of, for our money;
And, though fowle, now, be scarce, yet there are clarkes,
The skie not falling, thinke we may have larkes.
He tell your more, and lye, so you will come:
Of partrich, pheasant, wood-cock, of which some
May yet be there; and godwit, if we can:
Knat, raile, and ruffe too. How so ere, my man
Shall reade a piece of Virgil, Tacitus,
Livie, or of some better booke to us,
Of which wee'll speake our minds, amidst our meate;
And Ile professe no verses to repeate:
To this, if ought appeare, which I not know of,
That will the pastrie, not my paper, show of
Digestive cheese, and fruit there sure will bee;
But that, which most doth take my Muse, and mee,
Is a pure cup of rich Canary-wine,
Which is the Mermaids, now, but shall be mine:
Of which had Horace, or Anacreon tasted,
Their lives, as doe their lines, till now had lasted.
Tabacco, Nectar, or the Thespian spring,
Are all but Luthers beere, to this I sing.
Of this will have no Pooly', or Parrot by;
Nor shall our cups make any guiltie men:
But, at our parting, we will be, as when
We innocently met. No simple word,
That shall be utter'd at our mirthfull boord,
Shall make us sad next morning: or affright

The libertie, that wee'll enjoy to night.

(Ben Jonson)*

* I am grateful to my colleague, Paul Merchant, for drawing these examples to my attention.

It is obvious that the three English poems are very different from one another, visually different in terms of length, shape, organization of lines, and enormously different in tone. What they have in common is what Popovič describes as the invariant core, elements such as *the invitation to dinner* line, the *affectionate joky tone* line and the *plea of poverty* line. What is missing in the third version, however, is the other consistent element in the original and the two English versions, the *compliment to Lesbia* line. The invariant therefore comprises both theme and tone, for the forms and approaches employed by the translators are widely different. Marris has clearly attempted a 'close' translation, in so far as the bounds of English syntax and the formal structures of rhyme and metre allow, but the method is so restrictive that by line 10 it has begun to obscure the meaning and blunt the sharpness of the poem. Catullus's skill depends on compressing a large amount of information into a small frame, of writing a poem that is sumultaneously a gently comic invitation to a friend and a token of appreciation of the woman he loves. Moreover, it relies on the familiarity of the reader with a set of referential systems – the joke about the gods, for example, or the significance of perfume, which mean nothing to the contemporary reader. Marris, however, chooses to translate the words even though the references may be obscure, but opts for a curiously archaic formulation of lines 11 and 12. He uses the term *essence* rather than *perfume*, and translates *meae puellae* grandly as *to my lady,* retaining the plural form of *Veneres Cupidinesque* although the significance of that plural is lost on English readers. Then in the last two lines he runs into other difficulties. By translating *tu olfacies* as *sniff it*, he alters the register, and then returns immediately in the second part of the line to more courtly language but this time with all the connotations of the term *heaven* as opposed to *god*, by which he chooses to translate *deos*. One is left wondering exactly what Marris' criteria for choosing to translate this poem must have been. Had he merely wanted to transmit the content of the original to English readers he would have been content with paraphrase, so clearly he was concerned to create an English poem. He seems to have fallen into the pitfalls awaiting the translator who decides to tie himself to a very formal rhyme scheme in the TL version, at the expense, in this case, of giving the English poem any force and substance.

Frank Copley's criteria, on the other hand, are quite clear. He has focused on the joky, conversational tone of the original, on the close friendship between the speaker and the addressee that emerges from the poem and has updated the language in an attempt to ensure that the characterization of the speaker predominates over all the other elements. His version is a dramatic monologue in a kind of Damon Runyonesque dialect, but he gets much nearer to the original than the Marris version on several counts. His opening, *Say, Fabullus*, has the instant impact of Catullus' opening line, as opposed to the formal first line of the Marris version where the friendship element is placed after *so please the gods* and is consequently distanced. Copley's insertions and additions to the Catullus are deliberate attempts to clarify points that may be obscure to the twentieth-century reader – so the line from the song, followed immediately by *no*? is a means of linking the two parts of the poem that seem so unevenly matched in the Marris version. However, the *VENUS and CUPID LTD.* phrase is an attempt at clarification by use of a different method. Here the original joke relying on the plural form has been transposed into another system of humour, and the joke now derives from the use of the gods' names in a deviant context.

The Copley version, then, far from being an aberration of the original, in some respects comes closer to the Latin poem than the more literal version by Marris. As Popovič has pointed out, the fact that the process of translation may involve shifts in the semantic properties of the text does not mean that the translator wanted to underemphasize the semantic appeal of the original but rather because the translator

> is endeavouring to convey the semantic substance of the original in spite of the differences separating the system of the original from that of the translation, in spite of the differences between the two languages and between the two methods of presenting the subject matter.[14]

But Copley's version is harder to justify when the register of his poem is compared to that of the Catullus poem. Catullus, after all, was an aristocrat, whose language, although flexible, is elegant, and Copley's speaker is a caricature of a teenager from the Johnny Ray generation. Copley's choice of register makes the reader respond in a way that downgrades the material itself. The poem is no longer a rather suave and sophisticated mingling of several elements, it is located very precisely in a specific time and context. And, of course, in the relatively short time since the translation appeared, its language and tone have become almost as remote as that of the original!

   The third version is very obviously not a close translation of Catullus' *Poem 13* and yet at the same time it comes nearer in mood, tone and language to Catullus than either of the other versions. Compare the gently mocking

> haec, si, inquam, attuleris, venuste noster,
> cenabis bene;

to

> And, though fowle, now, be scarce, yet there are clarkes,
> The skie not falling, thinke we may have larkes.

The plea of poverty, the affection between the two friends, the contrast between what is projected as the ideal dinner and what is the possible dinner, all these elements are beautifully expressed by Jonson. The compliment to the lady has vanished, in its place is the love of learning; the perfume has been replaced with a Canary-wine that would have bestowed eternal life on Horace or Anacreon in person. The two sections of the poem, perfectly maintained, have nevertheless been utilized differently by the poet. Jonson's poem is a fine example of what Ludskanov describes as *semiotic transformation* (see p. 18) or *creative transposition* in Jakobson's terms, for he has taken Catullus' poem and worked outwards from it to give it a new life in the context of Renaissance England.

But there is another element in Jonson's poem, that raises again the whole question of intertextuality. The humour system within the poem is accessible to any reader, but to the reader already familiar with Catullus' poem a second system of humour comes into play. So the translator putting the Jonson poem into German, for example, would miss a great deal if he did not take into account the relationship between the English and the Latin poems, and the syntactical echoes by which Jonson deliberately recalls his source text for the discerning reader. Jonson's poem, then, may be read in its own right *and* in its relationship to Catullus.

Michael Rifaterre, in his book *Semiotics of Poetry,* argues that the reader is the only one who makes the connections between text, interpretant and intertext and suggests that

> The reader's manufacture of meaning is thus not so much a progress through the poem and a half-random accretion of verbal associations, as it is a seesaw scanning of the text, compelled by the very duality of the signs – ungrammatical as mimesis, grammatical within the significance network.[15]

He goes on to suggest that in the reader's mind there is a process of 'continual recommencing', and *indecisiveness* alternately lost and recovered with each reliving of 'revealed significance'. He claims that it is this fluctuation that makes a poem endlessly readable and fascinating. Yet clearly if he is right about the way in which a reader approaches a poem – and at the start of his book he claims that layers of meaning only emerge from *several* readings – then this thesis reinforces the argument against the one absolute, inflexible translation and against the desirability of the close translation which is, after all, merely one restricted reading of a poem.

With the three versions of the Catullus poem above, it was possible to see how the closer the translation came to trying to recreate *linguistic* and *formal* structures of the original, the further removed it became in terms of function. Meanwhile, huge deviations of form and language managed to come closer to the original intention. But this is not the only criterion for the translation of poetry, and a consideration of two attempts to translate the Anglo-Saxon poem, *The Seafarer*, will reveal a very different set of principles. Because of the length of the poem, I have restricted the discussion to selected passages (for the original, see Appendix).

The Seafarer

(1)   A song I sing   of my sea-adventure,
        The strain of peril,   the stress of toil,
        Which oft I endured   in anguish of spirit
        Through weary hours   of aching woe.
        My bark was swept   by the breaking seas;
        Bitter the watch   from the bow by night
        As my ship drove on   within sound of the rocks.
        My feet were numb   with the nipping cold,
        Hunger sapped   a sea-weary spirit,
        And care weighed heavy   upon my heart.
            Little the landlubber,   safe on shore,
        Knows what I've suffered   in icy seas
        Wretched and worn   by the winter storms,
        Hung with icicles,   stung by hail,
        Lonely and friendless   and far from home.
        In my ears no sound   but the roar of the sea,
        The icy combers,   the cry of the swan;
        In place of the mead-hall   and laughter of men
        My only singing   the sea-mew's call,
        The scream of the gannet,   the shriek of the gull;
        Through the wail of the wild gale   beating the bluffs
        The piercing cry   of the ice-coated petrel,

The storm-drenched eagle's   echoing scream.
In all my wretchedness,   weary and lone,
I had no comfort   of comrade or kin.
   Little indeed can he credit,   whose town-life
Pleasantly passes   in feasting and joy,
Sheltered from peril,   what weary pain
Often I've suffered   in foreign seas.
Night shades darkened   with driving snow
From the freezing north,   and the bonds of frost
Firm-locked the land,   while falling hail,
Coldest of kernels,   encrusted earth.
   Yet still, even now,   my spirit within me
Drives me seaward   to sail the deep,
To ride the long swell   of the salt sea-wave.
Never a day   but my heart's desire
Would launch me forth   on the long sea-path,
Fain of far harbors   and foreign shores.
Yet lives no man   so lordly of mood,
So eager in giving,   so ardent in youth,
So bold in his deeds,   or so dear to his lord,
Who is free from dread   in his far sea-travel,
Or fear of God's purpose   and plan for his fate.
The beat of the harp,   and bestowal of treasure,
The love of woman,   and worldly hope,
Nor other interest   can hold his heart
Save only the sweep   of the surging billows;
His heart is haunted   by love of the sea.
   Trees are budding   and towns are fair,
Meadows kindle   and all life quickens,
All things hasten   the eager-hearted,
Who joy therein,   to journey afar,
Turning seaward   to distant shores.
The cuckoo stirs him   with plaintive call,
The herald of summer,   with mournful song,
Foretelling the sorrow   that stabs the heart.
Who liveth in luxury,   little he knows
What woe men endure   in exile's doom.
   Yet still, even now,   my desire outreaches,

My spirit soars   over tracts of sea,
O'er the home of the whale,   and the world's expanse.
Eager, desirous,   the lone sprite returneth;
It cries in my ears   and it urges my heart
To the path of the whale   and the plunging sea.

(Charles W. Kennedy)

The Seafarer

(2)   May I for my own self song's truth reckon,
Journey's jargon, how I in harsh days
Hardship endured oft.
Bitter breast-cares have I abided,
Known on my keel many a care's hold,
And dire sea-surge, and there I oft spent
Narrow nightwatch nigh the ship's head
While she tossed close to cliffs.   Coldly afflicted,
My feet were by frost benumbed.
Chill its chains are; chafing sighs
Hew my heart round and hunger begot
Mere-weary mood.   Lest man know not
That he on dry land loveliest liveth,
List how I, care-wretched, on ice-cold sea,
Weathered the winter, wretched outcast
Deprived of my kinsmen;
Hung with hard ice-flakes, where hail-scur flew,
There I heard naught save the harsh sea
And ice-cold wave, at whiles the swan cries,
Did for my games the gannet's clamour,
Sea-fowls' loudness was for me laughter,
The mews' singing all my mead-drink.
Storms, on the stone-cliffs beaten, fell on the stern
In icy feathers;   full oft the eagle screamed
With spray on his pinion.
         Not any protector
May make merry man faring needy.
This he little believes, who aye in winsome life
Abides 'mid burghers some heavy business,

Wealthy and wine-flushed, how I weary oft
Must bide above brine.
Neareth nightshade, snoweth from north,
Frost froze the land, hail fell on earth then,
Corn of the coldest.   Nathless there knocketh now
The heart's thought that I on high streams
The salt-wavy tumult traverse alone
Moaneth alway my mind's lust
That I fare forth, that I afar hence
Seek out a foreign fastness.
For this there's no mood-lofty man over earth's midst,
Not though he be given his good, but will have in his
                                              youth greed;
Nor his deed to the daring, nor his king to the faithful
But shall have his sorrow for sea-fare
Whatever his lord will.
He hath not heart for harping, nor in ring-having
Nor winsomeness to wife, nor world's delight
Nor any whit else save the wave's slash,
Yet longing comes upon him to fare forth on the water
Bosque taketh blossom, cometh beauty of berries,
Fields to fairness, land fares brisker,
All this admonisheth man eager of mood,
The heart turns to travel so that he then thinks
On flood-ways to be far departing.
Cuckoo calleth with gloomy crying,
He singeth summerward, bodeth sorrow,
The bitter heart's blood.   Burgher knows not –
He the prosperous man – what some perform
Where wandering them widest draweth.
So that but now my heart burst from my breastlock,
My mood 'mid the mere-flood,
Over the whale's acre, would wander wide.
On earth's shelter cometh oft to me,
Eager and ready, the crying lone-flyer,
Whets for the whale-path the heart irresistibly,
O'er tracks of ocean; seeing that anyhow

My lord deems to me this dead life
On loan and on land, I believe not
That any earth-weal eternal standeth
Save there be somewhat calamitous
That, ere a man's tide go, turn it to twain.
Disease or oldness or sword-hate
Beats out the breath from doom-gripped body.
And for this, every earl whatever, for those
speaking after –
Laud of the living, boasteth some last word,
That he will work ere he pass onward,
Frame on the fair earth 'gainst foes his malice,
Daring ado, . . .
So that all men shall honour him after
And his laud beyond them remain 'mid the English,
Aye, for ever, a lasting life's blast,
Delight 'mid the doughty,
      Days little durable,
And all arrogance of earthen riches,
There come now no kings nor Caesars
Nor gold-giving lords like those gone.
Howe'er in mirth most magnified,
Whoe'er lived in life most lordliest,
Drear all this excellence, delights undurable!
Waneth the watch, but the world holdeth.
Tomb hideth trouble. The blade is layed low.
Earthly glory ageth and seareth.
No man at all going the earth's gait,
But age fares against him, his face paleth,
Grey-haired he groaneth, knows gone companions,
Lordly men, are to earth o'ergiven,
Nor may he then the flesh-cover, whose life ceaseth,
Nor eat the sweet nor feel the sorry,
Nor stir hand nor think in mid heart,
And though he strew the grave with gold,
His born brothers, their buried bodies
Be an unlikely treasure hoard.
                              (Ezra Pound)

First, there is the question of determining what the poem is about: is it a dialogue between an old sailor and a youth, or a monologue about the fascination of the sea in spite of the hardships endured by the sailor? Should the poem be perceived as having a Christian message as an integral feature, or are the Christian elements additions that sit uneasily over the pagan foundations? Second, once the translator has decided on a clear-cut approach to the poem, there remains the whole question of the form of Anglo-Saxon poetry; its reliance on a complex pattern of stresses within each line, with the line broken into two half-lines and rich patterns of alliteration running through the whole. Any translator must first decide what constitutes the total structure (i.e. whether to omit Christian references or not) and then decide on what to do when translating a type of poetry which relies on a series of rules that are non-existent in the TL.

Charles Kennedy's translation is restricted to the first 65 lines of the 108 lines of the poem, whilst Ezra Pound's translation comprises 101 lines and, since he omits the conclusion, he is compelled to make alterations to the main body of the text to ensure that all possible Christian significance is removed. So ll. 73–81 in Pound's version read as follows:

> And for this, every earl whatever, for those speaking after –
> Laud of the living, boasteth some last word,
> That he will work ere he pass onward,
> Frame on the fair earth 'gainst foes his malice,
> Daring ado . . .
> So that all men shall honour him after
> And his laud beyond them remain 'mid the English,
> Aye, for ever, a lasting life's blast,
> Delight 'mid the doughty,

The extent to which Pound has altered the text can be seen when his passage is set against a literal translation:

> Wherefor the praise of living men who shall speak after he is gone, the best of fame after death for every man, is that he should strive ere he must depart, work on earth with

bold deeds against the malice of fiends, against the devil, so
that the children of men may later exalt him and his praise
live afterwards among the angels for ever and ever, the joy
of life eternal, delight amid angels.[16]

Hence *deofle togeanes* (against the devil) is omitted in l. 76
mid englum (among the angels) becomes *'mid the English,*
dugeþum (angel hosts) become *the doughty*. In an even greater shift, the translation of *eorl* (man) by the specific *earl*
further serves to focus Pound's poem on the suffering of a
great individual rather than on the common suffering of
everyman. The figure that emerges from Pound's poem is a
grief-stricken exile, broken but never bowed, who draws the
comparison between his own lonely life at sea and the man

> who aye in winsome life
> Abides 'mid burghers some heavy business,
> Wealthy and wine-flushed,

But the figure who is portrayed in Charles Kennedy's version,
a figure who mitigates the aggressive repetition of *I* with the
more personal object pronoun *me* and the possessive *my*, is a
Ulysses-type, urged forward by outreaching desire. The concluding lines of Kennedy's version show the Ulysses figure
driving himself onwards, and the deliberate translation of *gifre*
(unsatisfied) by the positive *eager* (which Pound copies) alters
the balance of the poem in favour of the Seafarer as an *active*
character:

> Eager, desirous,   the lone sprite returneth;
> It cries in my ears   and it urges my heart
> To the path of the whale   and the plunging sea.

There is a large body of literature on the question of the
accuracy of Pound's translation and it would be possible to
consider Kennedy's version within the terms of the same
debate. But as Pound declared with his *Homage*, it was not his
intention to produce a crib and clearly a close comparison
between the original and his translation of *The Seafarer* reve-

als an elaborate set of word games that show the extent of his knowledge of Anglo-Saxon rather than his ignorance of that language. It seems fair to say, therefore, that linguistic closeness between SL and TL was not a prime criterion for Pound. In Kennedy's poem there are fewer major deviations from the original, but closeness should not be regarded as a more central criterion either. In an attempt to arrive at some idea of what criteria are employed in both versions, the following table provides a rough guide:

Pound	*Kennedy*
(1) Free-verse format.	Preservation of visual appearance of original by use of half-line format.
(2) Illusion of preservation of Anglo-Saxon stress pattern broken by irregular lines in TL text.	Attempt to preserve regular stress pattern even at risk of monotony in TL.
(3) Complex patterns of alliteration set up superficially similar to original.	Less complex patterns of alliteration.
(4) Attempt at mock-Germanic syntax-inversion, compounded words, archaisms, e.g. *mood-lofty man* (l. 40), *bosque taketh blossom* (l. 49), *any earth-weal eternal standeth* (l. 68).	Some inversion, some compounding, e.g. *sea-wave* (l. 36), *eager-hearted* (l. 52).
(5) No attempt to modernize language, resulting in poem where language and syntax are	Use of twentieth-century language, e.g. *landlubber* (l. 11),

consistently archaic and 'strange'.	I've (l. 12), persistent use of object pronouns with archaisms, resulting in uneven language.
(6) Attempt to reproduce *sounds* of original.	No deliberate attempt to reproduce sounds of original.
(7) Poem conceived as non-Christian. Stress on pre-Christian Germanic values of strength and resilience. Final lines omitted, all references to God, after-life, etc. omitted or changed.	Poem conceived as study of an exiled individual. No attempt to eliminate religious references (see God, l. 44) but decision to only translate one part of poem avoids almost all problems in this respect.
(8) Poem attempts to show individual in a world-system distanced in time, space and values.	Poem attempts to relate Anglo-Saxon world to that of contemporary reader.
(9) Poem attempts to provide 'flavour' of Anglo-Saxon verse through fiction of reproducing Anglo-Saxon form, language and sound patterns in TL.	Poem does not deliberately attempt to reproduce Anglo-Saxon 'flavour'.
(10) Poem attempts to reproduce elegiac mood of original.	The same.

This table is by no means comprehensive, but it does serve to show some of the criteria that can be determined from analysis of the translations. Pound's version appears to be the more complex of the two, because he seems to be trying to operate on more levels than Kennedy, but both poets very definitely use the SL text as a starting point from which to set out and construct a poem in its own right with its own system of meaning. Their translations are based on their *interpretation* of the original and on their *shaping* of that interpretation.

It has often been argued, in accordance with Longfellow (see p. 70), that *translation* and *interpretation* are two separate activities, and that it is the duty of the translator to translate what is there and not to 'interpret' it. The fallacy of such an argument is obvious – since every reading is an interpretation, the activities cannot be separated. James Holmes has devised the following useful diagram to show the interrelationship between translation and critical interpretation:[17]

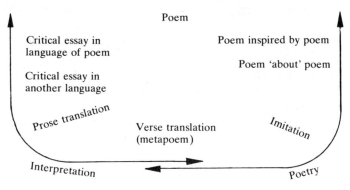

The verse translation rests on the axis point where types of interpretation intersect with types of imitation and derivation. Moreover, a translator will continue to produce 'new' versions of a given text, not so much to reach an ideal 'perfect translation' but because each previous version, being context bound, represents a reading accessible to the time in which it is produced, and moreover, is individualistic. William Morris' versions of Homer or of *Beowulf* are both idiosyncratic in that they spring from Morris' own system of priorities and com-

mitment to archaic form and language, and they are Victorian
in that they exemplify a set of canons distinctive to one period
in time. The great difference between a text and a metatext is
that the one is *fixed* in time and place, the other is *variable*.
There is only one *Divina Commedia* but there are innumerable readings and in theory innumerable translations.

The translations of *The Seafarer* and the Catullus poem
discussed above illustrate some of the complexities involved in
the translation of poetry where there is a gulf between the SL
and TL cultures through distance in time and space. All the
translations reflect the individual translators' readings,
interpretations and selection of criteria determined by the
concept of the *function* both of the translation and of the
original text. So from the poems examined we can see that in
some cases *modernization* of language and tone has received
priority treatment, whilst in other cases conscious archaiza-
tion has been a dominant determining feature. The success or
failure of these attempts must be left to the discretion of the
reader, but the variations in method do serve to emphasize the
point that there is no single *right* way of translating a poem just
as there is no single right way of writing one either.

So far the two poems discussed have belonged to remote
systems. When we consider the question of translating a contemporary writer, in this case a poem by Giuseppe Ungaretti
(1888–1970), other issues arise. The poem is typical of
Ungaretti's work in that it is as linear and bare as a Brancusi
sculpture and extremely intense through its apparent simplicity:

Vallone, 20 April 1917

Un'altra notte,
In quest'oscuro
colle mani
gelate
distinguo
il mio viso

Mi vedo
abbandonato nell'infinito

Typical of Ungaretti, also, is the spatial arrangement of the poem, a vital intrinsic part of the total structure, which interacts with the verbal system to provide the special grammar of the poem's own system. For the translator, then, the spatial arrangement of the SL text must be taken into account but in the two versions below it is clear that some variation has taken place.

(A)	In this dark with frozen hands I make out my face	(B)	In this dark with hands frozen I make out my face
	I see myself adrift in infinite space. (Patrick Creagh)		I see myself abandoned in the infinite. (Charles Tomlinson)

In version A there are only six lines, as opposed to the seven lines of the original and of version B, and this is due to the deliberate regularizing of the English syntax in l.2. Version B, however, distorts the TL syntax in order to keep the adjective *frozen* in a separate position in l.3 parallel to *gelate*. But this distortion of syntax, which produces an effect totally different from that of the original, comes from a deliberate decision to use Italian norms in English language structures. Whereas the strength of the original depends on the *regularity* of the word order, the English text relies on *strangeness*.

The problem of spatial arrangement is particularly difficult when applied to free verse, for the arrangement itself is meaningful. To illustrate this point, if we take Noam Chomsky's famous 'meaningless' sentence: *Colourless green ideas sleep furiously* and arrange it as

Colourless
green ideas
   sleep

furiously

the apparent lack of logical harmony between the elements of the sentence could become acceptable, since each 'line' would add an idea and the overall meaning would derive from the association of illogical elements in a seemingly logical regular structure. The meaning, therefore, would not be *content bound*, but would be *sign bound*, in that both the individual words and the association of ideas would accumulate meaning as the poem is read.

The two translations of the Ungaretti poem make some attempt to set out a visual structure that accords with the original, but the problems of the distance between English and Italian syntax loom large. Both English versions appear to stress the *I* pronoun, because Italian sentence structure is able to dispense with pronouns in verbal phrases. Both opt for the translation *make out* for *distinguo*, which alters the English register. The final line of the poem, deliberately longer in the SL version, is rendered longer also in both English versions, but here there is substantial deviation between the two. Version B keeps closely to the original in that it retains the Latinate *abandoned* as opposed to the Anglo-Saxon *adrift* in version A. Version B retains the single word *infinite*, that is spelled out in more detail in version A with *infinite space*, a device that also adds an element of rhyme to the poem.

The apparent simplicity of the Italian poem, with its clear images and simple structure conceals a deliberate recourse to that process defined by the Russian Formalists as *ostranenie*, i.e. making strange, or consciously thickening language within the system of the individual work to heighten perception (see Tony Bennet, *Formalism and Marxism*, London 1979). Seen in this light, version A, whilst pursuing the 'normalcy' of Ungaretti's linguistic structures, loses much of the power of what Ungaretti described as the 'word-image'. Version B, on the other hand, opts for a higher tone or register, with rhetorical devices of inverted sentence structure and the long, Latinate final line in an attempt to arrive at a 'thickened' language by another route.

In a brief but helpful review-article on translation Terry

Eagleton notes that much discussion has centred on the notion that the text is a given datum and that 'contention then centres on the operations (free, literal, recreative?) whereby that datum is to be reworked into another.' He feels, however, that one of the great gains of recent semiotic enquiry is that such a view is no longer tenable since the concept of intertextuality has given us the notion that every text is in a sense a translation:

> Every text is a set of determinate transformations of other, preceding and surrounding texts of which it may not even be consciously aware; it is within, against and across these other texts that the poem emerges into being. And these other texts are, in their turn, 'tissues' of such pre-existent textual elements, which can never be unravelled back to some primordial moment of 'origin'.[18]

It therefore becomes possible for a translator to see himself freed from the restrictions of those conventions governing translation that have prevailed at different moments in time and to treat the text responsibly as the starting point from which the metatext, or *translation-reading* (an interlingual reading) can begin. For as may be seen from the examples given above, all kinds of different criteria come into play during the translation process and all necessarily involve shifts of expression, as the translator struggles to combine his own pragmatic reading with the dictates of the TL cultural system. The reader may not *like* Frank Copley's 1950s-style Catullus, or Ezra Pound's mock-Anglo-Saxon poetry or Tomlinson's slightly lofty Ungaretti, but no one can argue that the translation products were not the result of a carefully determined concept of translation, conceived with a precise function in mind.

Before concluding this brief survey of some of the criteria governing the translation of poetry, I propose to look at one more text and two English versions, all distanced from the contemporary reader by several centuries. One interesting feature of these translations is that by choosing to retain, rather than replace, the form of the SL text, the translators encouraged a new form to enter the TL system; in this case, the sonnet.

> Amor, che nel penser mio vive e regna
> e 'l suo seggio maggior nel mio cor tène,
> talor armato ne la fronte vène,
> ivi si loca, et ivi pon sua insegna.
> Quella ch'amare e sofferir me 'nsegna
> e vol che 'l gran desio, l'accesa spene,
> ragion, vergogna e reverenza affrene,
> di nostro ardir fra se stessa si sdegna.
> Onde Amor paventoso fugge al core,
> lasciando ogni sua impresa, e piange, e trema;
> ivi s'asconde, e non appar più fore.
> Che poss'io far, temendo il mio signore,
> se non star seco in fin a l'ora estrema?
> ché bel fin fa chi ben amando more.
>
> (Francesco Petrarca)

> The longe love, that in my thought doeth harbar
>   And in myn hert doeth kepe his residence
>   Into my face preseth with bold pretence,
>   And therin campeth, spreding his baner.
> She that me lerneth to love and suffre
>   And will that my trust, and lustes negligence
>   Be rayned by reason, shame, and reverence
>   With his hardines taketh displeasure.
> Wherewithall, vnto the hertes forrest he fleith,
>   Leving his entreprise with payne and cry
>   And there him hideth and not appereth.
> What may I do when my maister fereth,
>   But, in the felde, with him to lyve and dye?
>   For goode is the liff, ending faithfully.
>
> (Sir Thomas Wyatt)

> Love that doth raine and live within my thought,
> And buylt his seat within my captyve brest,
> Clad in the armes wherein with me he fowght

Oft in my face he doth his banner rest.
But she that tawght me love and suffre paine,
My doubtfull hope and eke my hote desire
With shamfast looke to shadoo and refrayne,
Her smyling grace convertyth streight to yre.
And cowarde love than to the hert apace
Taketh his flight where he doth lorke and playne
His purpose lost, and dare not show his face.
For my lordes gylt thus fawtless byde I payne;
  Yet from my lorde shall not my foote remove.
  Sweet is the death that taketh end by love.
                   (Surrey)

The most striking aspect of any comparison of these three sonnets is the range of variation between them. Petrarch's sonnet splits into octet and sestet and follows the rhyme scheme a b b a/ a b b a/ c d c/ c d c. Wyatt's poem is similarly divided, but here the rhyme scheme is a b b a/ a b b a/ c d c/ c d d which serves to set the final two lines apart. Surrey's poem varies much more: a b a b/ c d c d/ e c e c/ f f and consists of three four-line sections building to the final couplet. The significance of these variations in form becomes clear once each sonnet is read closely.

Petrarch's poem opens with a conceit: Amor (Love), the lord and ruler of the Lover's heart is depicted as a military commander who raises his standard in the Lover's face, thus becoming visible. The first four lines, a single sentence, begin with the word *Amor* and end with Amor assertively showing his colours. With the next four lines there is a shift in perspective, and the focus is now on *Quella ch'amare e sofferir me 'nsegna* (She who teaches me to love and suffer). Again the four lines make up a single sentence, beginning with a description of the Lady's desire for the Lover to be ruled by reason, shame and reverence, and ending with the verb *si sdegna* (is displeased), the hinge phrase on which the poem pivots. The following tercet describes Amor's flight back to the heart, his fear of the Lady's displeasure and his subsequent hiding. But it is in the final tercet that the Lover speaks for himself, asking the reader a direct question that implies his own helplessness, bound as he is in a feudal relationship with his Lord, Amor. What can I do, he asks, since my Lord is afeared (and I fear him), except to stay with him to the final hour? and adds, in the last line, that he who dies loving well makes a good end.

The lover in Petrarch's poem is thus presented as timid, respectful, subordinate, both to the wishes of his Lady and to the commands of Love. He does not act but is acted upon, and the structure of the poem, with the first person singular verbal form only used at the end, and then only in a question that stresses his helplessness, reinforces this picture. The final line, an elaborate verbal conceit, emphasizes the virtues of passivity, or rather of the kind of passive love praised through the poem. But it is not enough to consider this poem in isolation, it must be seen as part of Petrarch's *Canzoniere* and linked therefore through language structures, imagery and a central shaping concept, to the other poems in the collection. Moreover, the attitude expressed by the lover in this poem (which links to the Petrarchan system that in turn is tied to the fourteenth-century vision of the role of loving and writing) should not be taken too literally at face value. The gentle ironic humour that emerges most clearly from the account of Amor's defeat and the Lover's powerlessness to do anything but follow him, offsets the serious moral principles behind the poem. The *voice* of the poem as a whole is thus distinct from the voice of the Lover.

Wyatt's translation undergoes a number of significant shifts, beginning in the first line with the addition of the adjective *longe* that detracts from the sharp personification of Petrarch's opening line. Moreover, whereas Amor 'lives and reigns', Wyatt's love 'in my thought doeth harbour'. It is in Surrey's version that the military language prevails, whilst Wyatt reduces the terminology of battle to a terminology of pageantry. With the second quartet there is another major shift – the Lady in Petrarch's sonnet is angered at the *joint* boldness of Amor and the Lover (*di nostro ardir* – at our boldness) whereas Wyatt's Lady is displeased by 'his hardines'. In the description of Love's flight, Wyatt creates the image of 'the hertes forrest', and by using nouns 'with payne and cry', instead of verbs lessens the picture of total, abject humiliation painted by Petrarch.

It is in the final lines that the extent of the space between Wyatt and Petrarch becomes apparent. The Lover in Wyatt's poem asks a question that does not so much stress his helplessness as his good intentions and bravery. The Italian *temendo il mio signore* carries with it an ambiguity (either the Lord fears or the Lover fears the Lord, or, most probably, both) whilst Wyatt has stated very plainly that 'my master fereth'. The final line, 'For goode is the liff, ending faithfully' strengthens the vision of the Lover as noble. Whereas the Petrarchan lover seems to be describing the beauty of death through constant love, Wyatt's lover stresses the virtues of a good *life* and a faithful end. What emerges from Wyatt's poem is a portrait of an active Lover, brave and faithful, for whom the manifestation of love and the Lady's displeasure are not couched in militaristic terms at all. Love shows his colours and is repulsed and the Lover sets up the alternative ideal of a good life. We are in the world of politics, of the individual geared towards ensuring his survival, a long way from the pre-Reformation world of Petrarch.

Surrey's translation retains the military language of the SL text, but goes several stages further. The Lover is 'captyve', and he and Love have often fought. Moreover, the Lady is not in an unreachable position, angered by the display of Love. She is already won and is merely angered by what appears to be excessive ardour. Petrarch's sonnet mentions *desio* and *spene* (desire and hope) but Surrey's passion is presented in physical terms. Once the Lady has changed 'her smyling grace' to anger, Love flees, but his flight is decisively condemned by the Lover. 'Cowarde love' flies and in the safety of the heart he 'doth lurke and playne'. Moreover, in the final line of the third quartet, the Lover states plainly that he is 'fawtless' and suffers because of 'my lordes gylt'. The device of splitting the poem into three four-line stanzas can be seen as a way of reshaping the material content. The poem does not build to a question and a final line on the virtues of dying, loving well. It builds instead to a couplet in which the Lover states his determination not to abandon his guilty lord even in the face of death. The voice of the poem and the voice of the Lover are indistinguishable, and the stress on the I, apparent in Wyatt's poem already, is strengthened by those points in the poem where there is a clear identification with the Lover's position against the bad behaviour of the false lord Love.

Both the English translations, products of a socio-cultural system vastly different from that of Petrarch's time, subtly (and at times not so subtly) adjust the structural patterns and the patterns of meaning within the SL text. The shifts in Surrey's translation are such that he would seem to have been not only translating but deliberately repudiating those elements in the SL text of which he did not approve (e.g. the Lover's passivity, the impenetrable hierarchy that places the Lover on the lowest rung of the ladder). These would have had no place in a society which saw upward social movement as desirable. But Wyatt and Surrey's translations, like Jonson's Catullus translation, would have been read by their contemporaries *through* prior knowledge of the original, and those shifts that have been condemned by subsequent generations as taking something away from Petrarch, would have had a very different function in the circles of Wyatt and Surrey's cultured intellectual readership.

Translating prose

Although there is a large body of work debating the issues that surround the translation of poetry, far less time has been spent studying the specific problems of translating literary prose. One explanation for this could be the higher status that poetry holds, but it is more probably due to the widespread erroneous notion that a novel is somehow a simpler structure than a poem and is consequently easier to translate. Moreover, whilst we have a number of detailed statements by poet-translators regarding their methodology, we have fewer statements from prose translators. Yet there is a lot to be learned from determining the criteria for undertaking a translation, as has been demonstrated above.

For a number of years I have used an exercise designed to discover how the translation of a novel is approached. Students are asked to translate the opening paragraph(s) of any novel and the translations are then examined in group discussion. What has emerged from this exercise, time and again, is that students will frequently start to translate a text that they have not previously read or that they have read only once some time earlier. In short, they simply open the SL text and *begin at the beginning,* without considering how that opening section relates to the structure of the work as a whole. Yet it would be quite unacceptable to approach the translation of a poem in this way. This is significant because it shows that a different concept of the imaginary distinction between form and content prevails when the text to be considered is a novel. It seems to be easier for the (careless) prose translator to consider content as *separable* from form.

As an example of what can happen when the translator stresses content at the expense of the total structure, let us take the following extract; the opening of *The Magic Mountain*:

> An unassuming young man was travelling in midsummer, from his native city of Hamburg to Davos-Platz in the Canton of Grisons, on a three weeks' visit.
>
> From Hamburg to Davos is a long journey – too long, indeed, for so brief a stay. It crosses all sorts of country; goes up hill and down dale, descends from the plateaus of Southern Germany to the shores of Lake Constance, over its bounding waves and on across marshes once thought to be bottomless.
>
> (tr. H.T. Lowe-Porter)*

This fast-moving, energetic passage, consisting of three sentences with four verbs of action and movement pulls the

---

* I am grateful to my colleague, Tony Phelan, for bringing this example to my attention.

reader straight into the narrative. The no-nonsense details of the journey and the time of the young man's proposed stay combine with the authorial value judgement on the brevity of the visit. In short, what we have here is a strong descriptive opening, with a powerful authorial presence, and the world picture painted here has close affinities with what the reader perceives as his own rational world.

The problem with this translation comes when it is set against the original German text, and the extent of the distance between the SL and the TL versions is compared. Mann's novel opens as follows:

> Ein einfacher junger Mensch reiste im Hochsommer von Hamburg, seiner Vaterstadt, nach Davos-Platz im Graubündischen. Er fuhr auf Besuch für drei Wochen.
>
> Von Hamburg bis dorthinauf, das ist aber eine weite Reise; zu weit eigentlich im Verhältnis zu einem so kurzen Aufenthalt. Es geht durch mehrerer Herren Länder, bergauf und bergab, von der süddeutschen Hochebene hinunter zum Gestade des Schwäbischen Meeres und zu Schiff über seine springende Wellen hin, dahin über Schlünde, die früher für unergründlich galten.

In this opening passage, the reader is given a series of clues that key him in to some of the codes operating through the novel. It is, of course, not restricted within the boundaries imposed by the realist world and depicts the ideological struggle between such dramatic opposites as health and sickness, life and death, democracy and reaction, and is set in a sanatorium where the characters are 'on holiday', removed from the struggle for existence. The journey depicted in the first few sentences is therefore functioning on more than one level: there is the young man's actual journey; the symbolic journey across a nation; the journey as a metaphor for the quest on which the reader is about to embark. Moreover, in Mann's description of the journey there are deliberate devices (e.g. the use of the classical term *Gestade* for *shore*) recalling eighteenth-century modes, for another major line through the novel is an attempt to bring together two stylistic modes, the lyrical and the prosaic. The English translator's compression of Mann's sentence structures reduces the number of levels on which the reader can approach the text, for clearly the translator's prime concern has been to create a sense of rapid movement. So the second sentence has been integrated with the first to form a single unit and the fourth sentence has been shortened by deliberate omissions (e.g. *zu Schiff* – by boat). The stylized terms describing places have been replaced by straightforward, geographical names and the stately language of Mann's text has been replaced with a series of clichés in a conversational account of an overly long journey.

There are also other variations. The introduction of the protagonist in Mann's first sentence in such deliberately decharacterized terms is yet another key to the reader, but by translating *einfacher* (ordinary) as *unassuming*, the English translator introduces a powerful element of characterization and alters the reader's perspective. And it is difficult not to conclude that the English translator has inadequately grasped the significance of the novel when there is even a case of mistranslation, *Schlünde* (abysses) rendered as *marshes*.

An example of a different kind of deviation through translation can be found by considering the following passages:

> Il primo di giugno dell'anno scorso Fontamara rimase per la prima volta senza illuminazione elettrica.   Il due di giugno, il tre di giugno, il quattro di giugno. Fontamara continuò a rimanere senza illuminazione elettrica.   Così nei giorni seguenti e nei mesi seguenti, finché Fontamara si riabituò al regime del chiaro di luna.   Per arrivare dal chiaro di luna alla luce elettrica, Fontamara aveva messo un centinaio di anni, attraverso l'olio di oliva e il petrolio.   Per tornare dalla luce elettrica al chiaro di luna bastò una sera.
>
> (*Fontamara,* I. Silone)

On the first of June last year Fontamara went without electric light for the first time.   Fontamara remained without electric light on the second, the third and the fourth of June.

So it continued for days and months. In the end Fontamara got used to moonlight again. A century had elapsed between the moonlight era and the electric era, a century which included the age of oil and that of petrol, but one evening was sufficient to plunge us back from electric light to the light of the moon.

(Fontamara, G. David and E. Mossbacher)

The opening passage of *Fontamara* introduces the reader immediately to the *tone* of the work, a tone that will remain through the device of the series of fictitious narrators whose accounts Silone is supposedly recording. And it is the tone, always downbeat and gently ironic even when the most moving and painful experiences are being described, that gives this novel its special quality. In the opening paragraph the narrator describes the transitoriness of progress, the way in which the long, slow development of technology that led to the arrival of electric light in a small mountain village can be overturned in a single night, and the faintly mocking, almost resigned tone is immediately established.

The Italian text consists of five sentences. The first two open with time phrases – *il primo di giugno* locates the start of the narrative on a definite date; *il primo di giugno* opens the sentence that expands on that initial blunt statement and moves the reader on in time. The third sentence again opens with a time phrase, now qualified by the conversational first word *cosi*, and moves still further into time future, through weeks and months. The final two sentences both open with a verbal phrase of movement: *per arrivare* and *per tornare*, that sum up the point being made in the opening paragraph about the slow movement of technological advancement compared to the speed with which that technology can be abandoned. The language of this paragraph is therefore misleadingly simple, and the almost conversational tone camouflages a heavily rhetorical passage, carefully structured to build to a point of climax and utilizing a series of patterns of repetition (e.g. the various time phrases; phrases such as *illuminazione elettrica, luce elettrica, chiaro di luna*, etc.).

The English translation has not made any attempt to retain the pattern of five sentences, beginning with either a time phrase or a verb of movement. Instead the second sentence inverts the time phrases, and puts them at the end – which could be defended in terms of English stylistic modes – and the remaining three sentences are formed by splitting one SL sentence into two and then by joining two other SL sentences together. This device works well in the first instance, creating the two short, conversational statements beginning '*So it continued*' and '*In the end*'. But by joining the two SL sentences into a single, long TL sentence, the sense of movement of the original is lost in the clumsy structure. The infinitives *arrivare* and *tornare* have become *elapsed* and *to plunge back*, the phrase *attraverso l'olio di oliva e il petrolio* has been expanded (but not made clearer) into *a century which included the age of oil and that of petrol*. The use of *era* strikes a jarring note, the inversion of the final part of the sentence means that all the impact of the last words of the SL text is lost, and the introduction of the personal pronoun *us* makes the shift in register between the first four sentences and the final one all the more incongruous. Yet there has clearly been an attempt to set up patterns of repetition in the English text (e.g. the repetition of *era, century*) even though phrases such as *chiaro di luna* and *luce elettrica* are not translated consistently. In short, it is difficult to see what the criteria behind the English translation were, for there are so many inconsistencies. What does seem apparent, however, is that the English translators have not given adequate consideration to the function of the stylistic devices used by Silone.

Wolfgang Iser, developing Roman Ingarden's discussion of the 'intentional sentence correlatives' that make up the world presented in the literary text,[19] points out that

> the intentional correlatives disclose subtle connections which individually are less concrete than the statements,

claims and observations, even though these only take on their real meaningfulness through the interaction of their correlatives.[20]

Iser goes on to state that the sentence does not consist solely of a statement 'but aims at something beyond what it actually says', since sentences within a literary text 'are always an indication of something that is to come, the structure of which is foreshadowed by their specific content'. If the translator, then, handles sentences for their specific content alone, the outcome will involve a loss of dimension. In the case of the English translation of the texts above, the sentences appear to have been translated at face value, rather than as component units in a complex overall structure. Using Popovič's terminology, the English versions show several types of *negative shift* involving:

(1) mistranslation of information;
(2) 'subinterpretation' of the original text;
(3) superficial interpretation of connections between intentional correlatives.

Having begun by stating that I intended to avoid value judgements of individual translations, it might now seem that I have deviated from my original plan. Moreover, it might seem unfair to lay so much emphasis on cases of negative shift that emerge from the first few sentences of a vast work. But the point that needs to be made is that although analysis of narrative has had enormous influence since Shlovsky's early theory of prose, there are obviously many readers who still adhere to the principle that a novel consists primarily of *paraphrasable material content* that can be translated straightforwardly. And whereas there seems to be a common consensus that a prose paraphrase of a poem is judged to be inadequate, there is no such consensus regarding the prose text. Again and again translators of novels take pains to create *readable* TL texts, avoiding the stilted effect that can follow from adhering too closely to SL syntactical structures, but fail to consider the way in which individual sentences form part of the total structure.

And in pointing out this failure, which is first and foremost a deficiency in reading, I believe that I am not so much passing judgement on the work of individuals as pointing towards a whole area of translation that needs to be looked at more closely.

Hilaire Belloc[21] laid down six general rules for the translator of prose texts:

(1) The translator should not 'plod on', word by word or sentence by sentence, but should 'always "block out" his work'. By 'block out', Belloc means that the translator should consider the work as an integral unit and translate in sections, asking himself 'before each what the whole sense is he has to render'.

(2) The translator should render *idiom by idiom* 'and idioms of their nature demand translation into another form from that of the original'. Belloc cites the case of the Greek exclamation 'By the Dog!', which, if rendered literally, becomes merely comic in English, and suggests that the phrase 'By God!' is a much closer translation. Likewise, he points out that the French historic present must be translated into the English narrative tense, which is past, and the French system of defining a proposition by putting it into the form of a rhetorical question cannot be transposed into English where the same system does not apply.

(3) The translator must render 'intention by intention', bearing in mind that 'the intention of a phrase in one language may be less emphatic than the form of the phrase, or it may be more emphatic'. By 'intention', Belloc seems to be talking about the weight a given expression may have in a particular context in the SL that would be disproportionate if translated literally into the TL. He quotes several examples where the weighting of the phrase in the SL is clearly much stronger or much weaker than the literal TL translation, and points out that in the translation of 'intention', it is often necessary to *add* words not in the

original 'to conform to the idiom of one's own tongue'.

(4) Belloc warns against *les faux amis*, those words or structures that may appear to correspond in both SL and TL but actually do not, e.g. *demander – to ask*, translated wrongly as *to demand*.

(5) The translator is advised to 'transmute boldly' and Belloc suggests that the essence of translating is 'the resurrection of an alien thing in a native body'.

(6) The translator should never embellish.

Belloc's six rules cover both points of technique and points of principle. His order of priorities is a little curious, but nevertheless he does stress the need for the translator to consider the prose text as a structured whole whilst bearing in mind the stylistic and syntactical exigencies of the TL. He accepts that there is a moral responsibility to the original, but feels that the translator has the right to significantly alter the text in the translation process in order to provide the TL reader with a text that conforms to TL stylistic and idiomatic norms.

Belloc's first point, in which he discusses the need for the translator to 'block out' his work, raises what is perhaps the central problem for the prose translator: the difficulty of determining *translation units*. It must be clear at the outset that the text, understood to be in a dialectical relationship with other texts (see *intertextuality* p. 79) and located within a specific historical context, is the prime unit. But whereas the poet translator can more easily break the prime text down into translatable units, e.g. lines, verses, stanzas, the prose translator has a more complex task. Certainly, many novels are broken down into chapters or sections, but as Barthes has shown with his methodology of five reading codes (see *S/Z*, discussed by T. Hawkes, *Structuralism and Semiotics*, London, 1977) the structuring of a prose text is by no means as linear as the chapter divisions might indicate. Yet if the translator takes each sentence or paragraph as a minimum unit and translates it without relating it to the overall work, he runs the risk of ending up with a TL text like those quoted above, where the paraphrasable content of the passages has been translated at the cost of everything else.

The way round this dilemma must once again be sought through considering the *function* both of the text and of the devices within the text itself. If the translators of Silone had considered the function of the tone they would have understood why the careful rhetorical patterning of the opening paragraph needed closer examination. Likewise, if the translator of Mann had considered the function of the description of both the young man and the journey, she would have understood the reasons for Mann's choice of language. Every prime text is made up of a series of interlocking systems, each of which has a determinable function in relation to the whole, and it is the task of the translator to apprehend these functions.

Let us consider as an example the problem of translating proper names in Russian prose texts, a problem that has bedevilled generations of translators. Cathy Porter's recent translation of Alexandra Kollontai's *Love of Worker Bees* contains the following note:

> Russians have a first ('Christian') name, a patronymic and a surname. The customary mode of address is first name plus patronymic, thus, Vasilisa Dementevna, Maria Semenovna. There are more intimate abbreviations of first names which have subtly affectionate, patronizing or friendly overtones. So for instance Vasilisa becomes Vasya, Vasyuk, and Vladimir becomes Volodya, Volodka, Volodechka, Volya.[22]

So the translator explains, quite properly, the Russian naming system, but this note is of little help during the actual reading process, for Cathy Porter retains the variations of name in the TL version and the English reader is at times confronted with the bewildering profusion of names on a single page all referring to the same character. In short, the SL system has been transported into the TL system, where it can only cause confusion and obstruct the process of reading. Moreover, as Boris

Uspensky has shown in his valuable book *A Poetics of Composition*,[23] the use of names in Russian can denote shifts in *point of view*. So in discussing *The Brothers Karamazov* Uspensky shows how the naming system can indicate multiple points of view, as a character is perceived both by other characters in the novel and from within the narrative. In the translation process, therefore, it is essential for the translator to consider the function of the naming system, rather than the system itself. It is of little use for the English reader to be given multiple variants of a name if he is not made aware of the function of those variants, and since the English naming system is completely different the translator must take this into account and follow Belloc's dictum to render 'idiom by idiom'.

The case of Russian proper names is only one example of the problem of trying to render a SL system into a TL that does not have a comparable system. Other examples might be found in the use by an author of dialect forms, or of regional linguistic devices particular to a specific region or class in the SL. As Robert Adams puts it, rather flippantly:

> Paris cannot be London or New York, it must be Paris; our hero must be Pierre, not Peter; he must drink an aperitif, not a cocktail; smoke Gauloises, not Kents; and walk down the rue du Bac, not Back Street. On the other hand, when he is introduced to a lady, he'll sound silly if he says, 'I am enchanted, Madame'.[24]

In the discussion of equivalence (see pp. 23–9) it was shown that any notion of *sameness* between SL and TL must be discounted. What the translator must do, therefore, is to first determine the *function* of the SL system and then to find a TL system that will adequately render that function. Levý posed the central questions that face the translator of literary prose texts when he asked:

> What degree of utility is ascribed to various stylistic devices and to their preservation in different types of literature . . .? What is the relative importance of linguistic standards

and of style in different types of literature . . .? What must have been the assumed quantitative composition of the audiences to whom translators of different times and of different types of texts addressed their translations?[25]

Translating dramatic texts

Whilst it seems that the bulk of genre-focused translation study involves the specific problem of translating poetry, it is also quite clear that theatre is one of the most neglected areas. There is very little material on the special problems of translating dramatic texts, and the statements of individual theatre translators often imply that the methodology used in the translation process is the same as that used to approach prose texts.

Yet even the most superficial consideration of the question must show that the dramatic text cannot be translated in the same way as the prose text. To begin with, a theatre text is read differently. It is read as something *incomplete*, rather than as a fully rounded unit, since it is only in performance that the full potential of the text is realized. And this presents the translator with a central problem: whether to translate the text as a purely literary text, or to try to translate it in its *function* as one element in another, more complex system. As work in theatre semiotics has shown, the linguistic system is only one optional component in a set of interrelated systems that comprise the *spectacle*. Anne Ubersfeld, for example, points out how it is impossible to separate *text* from *performance*, since theatre consists of the dialectical relationship between both, and she also shows how an artificially created distinction between the two has led to the literary text acquiring a higher status. One result of the supremacy of the literary text, she feels, has been the perception of performance as merely a 'translation':

> The task of the director, therefore, is to 'translate into another language' a text to which he has a prime duty to remain 'faithful'. This position is based on the concept of *semantic equivalence* between the written text and its performance; only the 'mode of expression' in the Hjelm-

slevian sense of the term will be altered, the form and content of the expression will remain identical when transferred from a system of test-signs to a system of performance-signs.[26]

As Ubersfeld shows, the danger with such an attitude is immediately obvious. The pre-eminence of the written text leads on to an assumption that there is a single *right* way of reading and hence performing the text, in which case the translator is bound more rigidly to a preconceived model than is the translator of poetry or prose texts. Moreover, any deviation, by director or translator, can be subjected to a value judgement that will assess both 'translations' as more or less deviant from the correct norm. A notion of theatre that does not see written text and performance as *indissolubly linked*, then, will inevitably lead to discrimination against anyone who appears to offend against the purity of the written text.

Moreover, the written text is a functional component in the total process that comprises theatre and is characterized in ways that distinguish it from a written text designed to be read in its own right. Jiří Veltrusky has shown how certain features of the written theatre text are distinctive, pointing out, for example, how dialogue unfolds both in time and in space and is always integrated in the extralinguistic situation, which comprises both the set of things that surround the speakers and the speakers themselves:

The relationship between the dialogue and the extra-linguistic situation is intense and reciprocal. The situation often provides the dialogue with its subject matter. Moreover, whatever the subject matter may be, the situation variously interferes in the dialogue, affects the way it unfolds, brings about shifts or reversals, and sometimes interrupts it altogether. In its turn, the dialogue progressively illuminates the situation and often modifies or even transforms it. The actual sense of the individual units of meaning depends as much on the extra-linguistic situation as on the linguistic context.[27]

And the dialogue will be characterized by rhythm, intonation patterns, pitch and loudness, all elements that may not be immediately apparent from a straightforward reading of the written text in isolation. Robert Corrigan, in a rare article on translating for actors,[28] argues that at all times the translator must *hear* the voice that speaks and take into account the 'gesture' of the language, the cadence rhythm and pauses that occur when the written text is spoken. In this respect, he is close to Peter Bogatyrev's concept of theatre discourse. Bogatyrev, discussing the function of the linguistic system in theatre in relation to the total experience declares that:

> Linguistic expression in theatre is a structure of signs con-
> stituted not only as discourse signs, but also as other signs.
> For example, theatre discourse, that must be the sign of a
> character's social situation is accompanied by the actor's
> gestures, finished off by his costumes, the scenery, etc.
> which are all equally signs of a social situation.[29]

But if the theatre translator is faced with the added criterion of *playability* as a prerequisite, he is clearly being asked to do something different from the translator of another type of text. Moreover, the notion of an extra dimension to the written text that the translator must somehow be able to grasp, still implies a distinction between the idea of the text and the performance, between the written and the physical. It would seem more logical, therefore, to proceed on the assumption that a theatre text, written with a view to its performance, contains distinguishable structural features that make it performable, beyond the stage directions themselves. Consequently the task of the translator must be to determine what those structures are and to translate them in to the TL, even though this may lead to major shifts on the linguistic and stylistic planes.

The problem of performability in translation is further complicated by changing concepts of performance. Consequently, a contemporary production of a Shakespearean text will be devised through the varied developments in acting style, playing space, the role of the audience and the altered concepts of tragedy and comedy that have taken place since Shakespeare's time. Moreover, acting styles and concepts of theatre also differ considerably in different national contexts, and this introduces yet another element for the translator to take into account.

As an example of some of the complexities involved in determining the criteria for the translation of a theatre text, let us consider the very vexed question of Racine, the French classical dramatist. A glance through the English translations immediately reveals one significant point – texts may have been translated singly (e.g. John Masefield's versions of *Esther* and *Berenice*) or as part of a volume of complete works (e.g. R.B. Boswell, the first translator of the Racinian *oeuvre*). This distinction shows straight away that whilst some texts may have been translated with performance in mind, others have been translated *without* such a precise notion. Arguably, the volume of 'complete plays' has been produced primarily for a reading public where literalness and linguistic fidelity have been principal criteria. But in trying to formulate any theory of theatre translation, Bogatyrev's description of linguistic expression must be taken into account, and the linguistic element must be translated bearing in mind its *function* in theatre discourse as a whole.

The difficulty of translating for the theatre has led to an accumulation of criticism that either attacks the translation as too literal and unperformable or as too free and deviant from the original. The leaden pedantry of many English versions of Racine, for example, is apt testimony to the fault of excessive literalness, but the problem of defining 'freedom' in a theatre translation is less easy to discern. In a short article[30] setting out some of the basic problems of translating theatre texts I quoted examples of translation shift where the problem lay in the deviation in *gestural patterning* between SL and TL, that resulted in dissolution in the TL of essential structures in the SL text. Ben Belitt's translation of Neruda's *Fulgor y Muerte de Joaquín Murieta*, mentioned previously (p. 78), is a good example of a case where the translator has altered the ideological basis of the text through over-emphasis of extralinguistic criteria – in this case, according to Belitt's own preface, the expectations of the American audience.

If we take the opening line of Racine's *Phèdre: Le dessein en est pris; je pars, cher Théramène,* a series of semantic, syntactic and stylistic problems immediately emerge, together with the added difficulties of considering the conventions of French classical theatre and the vastly different audiences of seventeenth-century France and twentieth-century England or America. Three English translators treat the line as follows:

> *I have resolved, Theramenes, to go.* (John Cairncross)
>
> *No, no, my friend, we're off.* (Robert Lowell)
>
> *No. No. I can't. I* can't. *How can I stay?* (Tony Harrison)

All three versions translate Hippolyte's intention to leave, but whilst the first two show the relationship between Hippolyte and his friend Théramène to be a key factor, the third does not. On the stylistic level, the first and the third versions follow the common practice of translating the French alexandrine into blank verse, since both have in common their pre-eminence as meters of classical theatre in their respective language systems. But in terms of theatre, only the second and third versions translate the *gestural understructure* of the French text, the rhythms contained within the language that determine patterns of physical gesture of the actor. Jean-Louis Barrault noted that the opening line of *Phèdre* matched the rhythms of Hippolyte's footsteps, ensuring that he was in position on the word Théramène.[31] There is an emphasis and determination in the SL line, stressed in both halves of the line and reaching its climax in the use of the name. Both the second and third English versions try to recreate that effect by using devices such as repetition and rhetorical question that both render the sense of the SL statement and reproduce a pattern of gesture. In short, the translation process has involved not only a sequence of linguistic transfers from SL to TL on the level of discourse signification, but also a transfer of the function of the linguistic utterance in relation to the other component signs of theatre discourse.

The first English version of Racine's *Andromache*, performed in 1674, appeared in print the following year together with an Epistle to the Reader by the man to whom the translation was generally attributed, John Crowne. In the Epistle, Crowne goes to some lengths to excuse the translation (claiming it to be the work of a 'Young Gentleman') and to explain why the production had not been a success. Crowne attributes the failure of the play not to the translation, although he admits that the English version had not bestowed 'Verse upon it', but to the expectations of the audience, accustomed to a given theatre tradition, who refused to respond to the 'thin Regalios' of the French theatre tradition. Yet less than forty years later Ambrose Phillips' version of *Andromache*, entitled *The Distres't Mother*, was such a success that it remained in repertoire right through the eighteenth century, with the leading role a favourite of most of the great English actresses of the period. What had Philips done to make such a triumph of a play judged earlier to be unsuited to English taste?

First, Phillips made substantial alterations to the play, shortening the text in places, adding speeches and, at the ends of Acts IV and V adding whole scenes, including a final scene in which the Distres't Mother prepares for a happy ending. This view of Racine's tragedy has led a number of critics to attack Philips' translation as deviant, but in his Preface Philips explains very clearly why he felt the need to adapt Racine:

> If I have been able to keep up to the Beauties of Monsieur *Racine* in my Attempt, and to do him no Prejudice in the Liberties I have taken frequently to vary from so great a Poet, I shall have no reason to be dissatisfied with the Labour it has cost me to bring the compleatest of his works upon the *English* stage.

Philips' principal criteria for translation appear to have been:

(1) *playability;*

(2) the relationship of the play to the established conventions of the theatre of his day (a theatre which restructured Shakespeare in the interests of canons and of decorum and good taste);
(3) clarity of the interrelationship between the characters.

Accepting that the careful balance of characters, scenes and speeches so basic to the original would have no significance in English – or, if it did, would seem heavy and contrived – Phillips chose to restructure the play for an English audience. In Act I sc. i, for example, the basis of Phillips' technique can be seen. In Racine, this first scene furnishes the audience with the basic information they will need to follow the plot (e.g. Oreste's love for Hermione, due to marry Pyrrhus, and Pyrrhus' love for the Trojan widow, Andromache). At the same time the scene introduces the fatal passion of Orcste with which the play will finally terminate. Pylade's role is to act as a foil to that passion, to provide the calming tones of reason. The balance of the scene hinges on the relationship between these two different types of men. Phillip's translation preserves both the function of the first scene in introducing the plot lines and the balance of the relationship between the two friends, but he has achieved this comparability not by following the surface structure of the SL text, but by recreating the deep structure of the scene in theatre terms. So, for example, Oreste's long monologue is broken up, since monologues of such length were not part of English stage convention; Pylade is given more lines and developed more fully as a friend rather than as a foil, since the device of the confidante was not so acceptable on the English stage. To use James Holmes' terminology, Phillips has established *a hierarchy of correspondences*[32] in which the written text is seen as an adaptable element in the production of live theatre.

A twentieth-century translation that follows similar criteria is Tony Harrison's version of *Phèdre, Phaedra Brittanica,* produced in 1976. In this translation Harrison has moved away from Greece, from the references to the gods, fate, the Minotaur – from the whole universe of myth out of which

Phèdre originated, and has substituted colonial India. And just as *Phèdre* deals with the coming together of disparate world systems – the passions of a doomed house and a world of order and rationality, in this vision of colonial India two similar worlds come into contact: the world of English order, so helpless in its new context, and the forces of darkness, typified by an alien culture in revolt against the colonizers. So in the final scene, where Racine's Phèdre confesses *Le ciel mit dans mon sein une flamme funeste,* the Memsahib of Harrison's text says *India put dark passions in my breast.* A good example of Harrison's technique may be found by comparing his version of the moment when Oenone (the Ayah) discovers Phèdre's secret passion with Robert Lowell's version of the same scene.

OENONE

Madame, au nom des pleurs que pour vous j'ai versés,
Par vos faibles genoux que je tiens embrassés,
Délivrez mon esprit de ce funeste doute.

PHÈDRE

Tu le veux.   Lève toi.

OENONE

Parlez, je vous écoute.

PHÈDRE

Ciel! que lui vais-je dire, et par où commencer?

OENONE

Par de vaines frayeurs cessez de m'offenser.

PHÈDRE

O haine de Vénus! O fatale colère!
Dans quels égarements l'amour jeta ma mère!

OENONE

Oublions-les, Madame; et qu'à tout l'avenir

Un silence éternel cache ce souvenir.

PHÈDRE

Ariane, ma soeur, de quel amour blessée,
Vous mourûtes aux bords où vous fûtes laissée!

OENONE

Que faites-vous, Madame? et quel mortel ennui
Contre tout votre sang vous anime aujourd'hui?

PHÈDRE

Puisque Vénus le veut, de ce sang déplorable
Je péris la dernière et la plus misérable.

OENONE

Aimez-vous?

PHÈDRE

De l'amour j'ai toutes les fureurs.

OENONE

Pour qui?

PHÈDRE

Tu vas ouïr le comble des horreurs.
J'aime . . . A ce nom fatal, je tremble, je frissonne,
J'aime . . .

OENONE

Qui?

PHÈDRE

Tu connais ce fils de l'Amazone,
Ce prince si longtemps par moi-même opprimé?

OENONE

Hippolyte? Grands Dieux!

PHÈDRE

C'est toi qui l'a nommé.

(Racine)

AYAH: (on her knees)
                   Memsahib, by these tears that wet your
                   dress
                   rid ayah of her anguish, and confess.

MEMSAHIB: (after a pause)
                   You wish it? Then I will. Up, off your
                   knees.
                   (pause)

AYAH: Memsahib made her promise. Tell me.
                   Please.

MEMSAHIB: I don't know what to say. Or how to start.
                   (pause)

AYAH: Tell me, Memsahib. You break my heart.

MEMSAHIB: (sudden vehemence)
                   Mother! Driven by the dark gods' spite
                   beyond the frontiers of appetite.
                   A *judge's* wife! Obscene! Bestialities
                   Hindoos might sculpture on a temple
                   frieze!

AYAH: Forget! Forget! The great wheel we are on
                   turns all that horror to oblivion.

MEMSAHIB: Sister! Abandoned . . . by him too . . . left
                   behind . . .
                   driven to drugs and drink . . . Out of her
                   mind!

AYAH: Memsahib, no. Don't let black despair
                   flail at your family. Forebear. Forebear.

MEMSAHIB: It's India! Your cruel gods athirst
                   for victims. Me the last and most accursed!

AYAH: (truth dawning)
                   Not love?

MEMSAHIB: Love. Like fever.
AYAH: Memsahib, whom?

MEMSAHIB:	Prepare to bear witness to the hand of doom.
	I love . . . I love . . . I love . . . You know the one
	I seemed to hate so much . . . the Rajput's son . . .
AYAH:	Thomas Theophilus? The half-breed! Shame!
MEMSAHIB:	I couldn't bring myself to speak his name.
	(Tony Harrison)

OENONE:	Ah Lady, I implore you by my tears,
	and by your suffering body. Heaven hears,
	and knows the truth already. Let me see.
PHAEDRA:	Stand up.
OENONE:	Your hesitation's killing me!
PHAEDRA:	What can I tell you? How the gods reprove me!
OENONE:	Speak!
PHAEDRA:	Oh Venus, murdering Venus! love
	gored Pasiphaë with the bull.
OENONE:	Forget
	your mother! When she died she paid her debt
PHAEDRA:	Oh Ariadne, Oh my Sister, lost
	for love of Theseus on that rocky coast.
OENONE:	Lady, what nervous languor makes you rave
	against your family; they are in the grave.
PHAEDRA:	Remorseless Aphrodite drives me. I,
	my race's last and worst love-victim, die.
OENONE:	Are you in love?
PHAEDRA:	I am with love!
OENONE:	Who
	is he?
PHAEDRA:	I'll tell you. Nothing love can do

	could equal. . . . Nurse, I am in love. The shame
	kills me. I love the . . .. Do not ask his name.
OENONE:	Who?
PHAEDRA:	Nurse, you know my old loathing for the son
	of Theseus and the barbarous Amazon?
OENONE:	Hippolytus! My God, oh my God!
PHAEDRA:	You,
	not I, have named him.

(Robert Lowell)

Here it is clear that Harrison has retained the essential movement of the scene, the Memsahib's brief anguished speeches
and the Ayah's desperate insistence that lead up to the climax
of the revelation, but he has substituted another system of
references for the Greek background, and has extended
Phèdre's lines to make the significance more explicit. The
connotations of the Memsahib's illicit passion are altered too;
in Harrison's play the taboo she violates is that of inter-racial
boundaries, not of incest. Yet the translation is contained
within the frame of a tight verse structure utilizing a form that
recalls Dryden rather than the usual blank verse. When compared to the Lowell translation, that uses the same form but
with far less flexibility, the gap between a *performance-
oriented* translation and a *reader-oriented* translation becomes
more clearly discernible.

Lowell expands Racine's text with explanations of the
mythological background that may be unclear to twentieth-
century readers. More significantly for the balance of the
scene, he gives Phaedra a series of speeches in which the
affirmative *I* is heavily stressed, whereas Harrison follows
Racine in making the Memsahib's speeches a combination of
direct addresses to her companion and thoughts voiced aloud.
Lowell even goes so far as to give Phaedra two additional
statements *I'll tell you* and *I am in love*. In short, although
Lowell seems at first glance to have followed Racine's text

more closely in terms of content material translated, it is Harrison who has most closely rendered the shifts in movement in the scene in spite of the obvious differences in the language.

With theatre translation, the problems of translating literary texts take on a new dimension of complexity, for the text is only one element in the totality of theatre discourse. The language in which the play text is written serves as a sign in the network of what Thadeus Kowzan calls *auditive* and *visual* signs.[33] And since the play text is written for voices, the literary text contains also a set of *paralinguistic* systems, where pitch, intonation, speed of delivery, accent, etc. are all signifiers. In addition, the play text contains within it the *undertext* or what we have called the *gestural text* that determines the movements an actor speaking that text can make. So it is not only the context but also the coded gestural patterning within the language itself that contributes to the actor's work, and the translator who ignores all systems outside the purely literary is running serious risks.[34]

Once again, as with other types of translation discussed in this book, the central issue concerns the *function* of the text to be translated. One of the functions of theatre is to operate on other levels than the strictly linguistic, and the role of the audience assumes a public dimension not shared by the individual reader whose contact with the text is essentially a private affair. A central consideration of the theatre translator must therefore be the performance aspect of the text and its relationship with an audience, and this seems to me not only to justify modifications of the kind made by Philips or Harrison to Racine's original text, but to suggest that the translator must take into account the function of the text as an element for and of performance.

CONCLUSION

I N writing the conclusion to this book I am constantly aware of the vast amount of material left undiscussed. For example, I have not mentioned the major developments in machine translation, that both contributed to advances in linguistics and then in turn benefited from those advances. The complex problems of translating cinematic texts, where the translation process also involves a kinetic-visual component as audiences focus on the lip movements of the actors, and the related question of subtitling, where reading speed, paraphrase and summary are integral elements, has not been dealt with at all. Nor, perhaps even more crucially, has the whole question of oral translation or interpreting been touched upon. It is easy to plead lack of space for such gaps, but I feel that nevertheless the point must be made so that this book may not seem to have a bias of the very kind it has sought to overcome: a bias towards 'high' literature that devalues work in the cinema, research in oral literature and electronics. Nothing could be further from my intentions, and in dealing with generally accepted 'literary' texts the central criterion was to acquaint the reader with the most widely discussed problems of translation.

Translation Studies, as stated in the Introduction, is still a young discipline and still has a long way to go. There is a need for more general theoretical discussion as to the *nature* of translation and a need for an accessible terminology with which to engage in such discussion. Anton Popovič's first attempt at a *Dictionary of Literary Translation Terminology* is to be applauded, but it needs streamlining and extending to cover discussion of theatre and cinematic texts. One great benefit to be derived from a more accessible terminology would be that we could move away from the old vague conflict between free and literal translation, with the attendant value judgements. We could also move away from the dubious distinction between author-directed and audience-directed translation.

We need to know much more about the history of Translation Studies. More documentation, more information about changing concepts of translation has become a priority and the establishment of an international collaborative venture on translation history, of the kind envisioned by James Holmes of Amsterdam, seems a logical way to proceed. By understanding more about the changing face of Translation Studies and the changing status of the translated text, we are better equipped to tackle the problems as they arise within our own contexts.

Within literary translation the work to be done is also glaringly obvious. There is a need for a comprehensive study of theatre translation with a view to establishing a theory, and there is a need for much more serious attention to be given to the specific problems of prose translation. André Lefevere's work on the methodological problems of translating poetry should be continued and extended, and the discussion of all types of literary translation will also be greatly advanced by a consideration of the problems of translating texts from outside Europe and the Americas.

But in listing some projects that need to be pursued further, it is important not to forget two key points: the enormous progress made so rapidly within the discipline itself and the interrelationship between scholarship and practice that still prevails. Roman Jakobson, discussing the complexities of translation, noted ironically that

> Both the practice and the theory of translation abound with intricacies, from time to time attempts are made to sever the Gordian knot by proclaiming the dogma of untranslatability.[1]

Indeed, that 'dogma' has often been used to argue for the impossibility not only of translation but also of Translation Study, on the grounds that it is not possible to discuss anything so tenuous as the transfer of the 'creative spirit' from language to language. Yet in spite of such a dogma, translators continue to translate, and the extended discussion that has begun with such promise can now be joined by anyone who, having encountered problems while translating, wants to move from a pragmatic, empirical position towards a more scientific, collaborative discourse.

NOTES

Introduction

1 A. Lefevere, 'Translation Studies: The Goal of the Discipline', in James S. Holmes, Josè Lambert and Raymond van den Broeck (eds), *Literature and Translation* (Louvain: ACCO, 1978), pp. 234–5. Lefevere has followed the lead set by James Holmes in his pamphlet, *The Name and Nature of Translation Studies*, pub. by Translation Studies Section, Univ. of Amsterdam, August 1975.

2 The abbreviations *SL – Source Language, TL – Target Language* will be used throughout.

3 Hilaire Belloc, *On Translation* (Oxford: The Clarendon Press, 1931).

4 In his article, 'Translation in the United States', *Babel* VII, (2), 1968, pp. 119–24 Henry Fischbach points out that the United States has a shorter history of translation than almost any other industrialized nation of the world, and attributes this deficiency to four basic points:

    (a) The political and commercial isolationism of nineteenth-century America.

    (b) The traditional cultural allegiance to the English-speaking community.

(c) The American complacent self-sufficiency in technology.

(d) The strength of the myth of the Land of Promise for emigrants and their subsequent desire to integrate.

Fischbach's theory is interesting in that it would seem to show correspondences with the English attitude towards translation linked to British colonial expansion.

5 Dante Gabriel Rossetti, Preface to his translations of Early Italian Poets, *Poems and Translations, 1850–1870* (London: Oxford University Press, 1968), pp. 175–9.

6 E. Fitzgerald, letter to Cowell, 20 March 1957.

7 Theodore Savory, *The Art of Translation* (London: Cape, 1957).

8 Eric Jacobsen, *Translation, A Traditional Craft* (Copenhagen: Nordisk Forlag, 1958).

9 Eugene Nida, *Toward a Science of Translating* (Leiden: E.J. Brill, 1964).

10 Horst Frenz, 'The Art of Translation' in N.P. Stallknecht and H. Frenz (eds), *Comparative Literature: Method and Perspective* (Carbondale: Southern Illinois University Press, 1961), pp. 72–96.

11 Anton Popovič, *Dictionary for the Analysis of Literary Translation* (Dept. of Comparative Literature, University of Alberta, 1976).

12 Randolph Quirk, *The Linguist and the English Language* (London: Edward Arnold, 1974).

13 J. Levý, *Umeni prekladu* (The Art of Translation) (Prague, 1963), cited in J. Holmes (ed.), *The Nature of Translation* (The Hague: Mouton, 1970).

14 J.C. Catford, *A Linguistic Theory of Translation* (London: Oxford University Press, 1965).

15 Lefevere, op. cit.

16 Francis Newman, 'Homeric Translation in Theory and Practice' in *Essays by Matthew Arnold* (London: Oxford University Press, 1914), pp. 313–77.

17 André Lefevere, *Translating Poetry, Seven Strategies and a Blueprint* (Amsterdam: Van Gorcum, 1975).

1 Central Issues

1 Edward Sapir, *Culture, Language and Personality* (Berkeley, Los Angeles: University of California Press, 1956), p. 69.

2 Jurí Lotman and B.A. Uspensky, 'On the Semiotic Mechanism of Culture', *New Literary History,* IX (2), 1978, pp. 211–32.

3 Roman Jakobson, 'On Linguistic Aspects of Translation', in R.A. Brower (ed.), *On Translation* (Cambridge, Mass.: Harvard University Press, 1959), pp. 232–9.

4 Georges Mounin, *Les problèmes théoriques de la traduction* (Paris: Gallimard, 1963).

5 Eugene Nida and Charles Taber, *The Theory and Practice of Translation* (Leiden: E.J. Brill, 1969), p. 484.

6 A. Ludskanov, 'A Semiotic Approach to the Theory of Translation', *Language Sciences,* 35 (April), 1975, pp. 5–8.

7 See Ferdinand de Saussure, *Course in General Linguistics* (London: Fontana, 1974).

8 Though there is also the idiomatic use of the phrase *bread and butter* that signifies basic essentials, means of livelihood, e.g. *to earn one's bread and butter.*

9 This sketch is taken from Eugene Nida, *Towards a Science of Translating. With Special Reference to Principles and Procedures Involved in Bible Translating* (Leiden: E.J. Brill, 1964), p. 107. All quotations from Nida, unless otherwise indicated, are taken from this volume.

10 J.R. Firth, *The Tongues of Men and Speech* (London: Oxford University Press, 1970), p. 110.

11 Popovič distinguishes several types of shift:

   (a) *Constitutive shift* (in translation) described as an inevitable shift that takes place as a result of differences between two languages, two poetics and two styles.

   (b) *Generic shift,* where the constitutive features of the text as a literary genre may change.

   (c) *Individual shift,* where the translator's own style and

idiolect may introduce a system of individual deviations.

(d) *Negative shift*, where information is incorrectly
translated, due to unfamiliarity with the language or
structure of the original.

(e) *Topical shift*, where topical facts of the original are
altered in the translation.

12 M.B. Dagut, 'Can Metaphor be Translated?' *Babel*, XXII
(1), 1976, pp. 21–33.

13 J.C. Catford, *A Linguistic Theory of Translation* (London:
Oxford University Press, 1965).

14 All quotations from Popovič, unless otherwise indicated,
are taken from his *Dictionary*.

15 Albrecht Neubert, 'Elemente einer allgemeinen Theorie
der Translation', *Actes du Xe Congrès International des
Linguistes,* 1967, Bucarest II, pp. 451–6.

16 See C.S. Pierce, *Collected Papers* (8 vols), ed. C.
Hartshorne, P. Weiss and A. Burks (Cambridge, Mass.:
Harvard University Press, 1931–58).
For a discussion of Pierce's contribution to semiotics, see
T. Hawkes, *Structuralism and Semiotics* (London:
Methuen, 1977), pp. 126–30.

17 One interesting aspect of languages in contact is that
systems of swearing and blasphemy often become
interchangeable. In the case of Chicano Spanish, the
Anglo-American system has been incorporated with the
traditional Spanish system.

18 Examples quoted by Raymond van den Broeck in 'The
Concept of Equivalence in Translation Theory: Some
Critical Reflections', in James S. Holmes, José Lambert
and Raymond van den Broeck (eds), *Literature and Translation* (Louvain: ACCO. 1978), pp. 29–48.

19 For a discussion of Lotman's theories, see D.W. Fokkema,
'Continuity and Change in Russian Formalism, Czech
Structuralism, and Soviet Semiotics', *PTL*, I (1) Jan.
1976, pp. 153–96, and Ann Shukman, 'The Canonization
of the Real: Jurí Lotman's Theory of Literature and

Analysis of Poetry', *PTL* I (2), April 1976, pp. 317–39.
20 Benjamin Lee Whorf, *Language, Thought and Reality* (Selected Writings) ed. J.B. Carroll (Cambridge, Mass.: The MIT Press, 1956), p. 213.
21 Lotman and Uspensky, op. cit.
22 J.L. Darbelnet and J.P. Vinay, *Stylistique comparée du français et de l'anglais* (Paris: Didier, 1958).
23 Boguslav P. Lawendowski, 'On Semiotic Aspects of Translation', in Thomas Sebeok (ed.), *Sight, Sound and Sense* (Bloomington: Indiana University Press, 1978), pp. 264–83.
24 Mounin, op. cit., p. 279.
25 Jiří Levý, *Die literarische Übersetzung. Theorie einer Kunstgattung,* tr. Walter Schamschula (Frankfurt am Main: Athenaion, 1969).
26 Octavio Paz, *Traducción: literatura y literalidad* (Barcelona: Tusquets Editor, 1971), p. 9.

2   History of translation theory

1 George Steiner, *After Babel* (London: Oxford University Press, 1975), pp. 236ff.
2 T.R. Steiner, *English Translation Theory, 1650–1800* (Assen and Amsterdam: Van Gorcum, 1975).
3 André Lefevere, *Translating Literature: The German Tradition. From Luther to Rosenzweig* (Assen and Amsterdam: Van Gorcum, 1977).
4 F.O. Matthiesson, *Translation. An Elizabethan Art* (Cambridge, Mass.: Harvard University Press, 1931). Quotations from North and Holland below are all taken from this text.
5 Timothy Webb, *The Violet in the Crucible* (London: Oxford University Press, 1976).
6 Eric Jacobsen, *Translation, A Traditional Craft* (Copenhagen: Nordisk Forlag, 1958).
7 Cicero, 'Right and Wrong', in *Latin Literature*, ed. M.

Grant (Harmondsworth: Penguin Books, 1978), pp. 42–3.

8 Cicero, *De optimo genere oratorum,* Loeb Classical Library, transl. H.M. Hubbell (London: Heinemann, 1959).

9 Horace, *On the Art of Poetry,* in *Classical Literary Criticism* (Harmondsworth: Penguin Books, 1965), pp. 77–97.

10 Longinus, *Essay On the Sublime,* in *Classical Literary Criticism* (Harmondsworth: Penguin Books, 1965), pp. 99–156.

11 There is a large body of literature on the history of Bible translation. Eugene Nida's *Towards a Science of Translating* (Leiden: E.J. Brill, 1964) contains a very extensive bibliography. There are also several works in English that provide useful introductions to the subject: F.F. Bruce, *The English Bible, A History of Translations* (London: Lutterworth Press, 1961). A.C. Partridge, *English Biblical Translation* (London: André Deutsch, 1973); W. Schwarz, *Principles and Problems of Biblical Translation: Some Reformation Controversies and their Background* (Cambridge: Cambridge University Press, 1955); H. Wheeler Robinson (ed.), *The Bible in its Ancient and English Versions* (Oxford: The Clarendon Press, 1940).

12 Erasmus, *Novum Instrumentum* (Basle: Froben, 1516). 1529, tr. W. Tindale.

13 Martin Luther, *Table Talks,* 1532. Both the quotations from Erasmus and Luther are taken from *Babel,* IX(1), 1970, a special issue on the translation of religious texts.

14 Alfred, Preface to Gregory's *Pastoral Care,* in G.L. Brook, *An Introduction to Old English* (Manchester: Manchester University Press, 1955).

15 See Jacobsen, op. cit., for details of the role of translations in the system of medieval training in rhetoric; also E. Curtius, *European Literature and the Latin Middle Ages* (London: Routledge & Kegan Paul, 1953).

16 Gianfranco Folena, 'Volgarizzare' e 'tradurre': idea e terminologia della traduzione dal Medio Evo italiano e

romanzo all'umanesimo europeo', in *La Traduzione. Saggi e studi* (Trieste: Edizioni LINT, 1973), pp. 57–120.

17 Chapman's *Homer*, ed. R. Heme Shepherd (London: Chatto & Windus, 1875).

18 E. Cary, *Les Grands Traducteurs Français* (Genève: Librairie de l'Université, 1963), pp. 7–8. This book contains a facsimile of Dolet's original 1540 pamphlet, *La manière de bien traduire d'une langue en aultre.*

19 George Steiner, op. cit., p. 247.

20 The quotations from Sir John Denham, Abraham Cowley and John Dryden are taken from texts reprinted in T.R. Steiner's book, op. cit.

21 J. Dryden, *The Aeneid*, IV (London: Oxford University Press, 1961), p. 212.

22 A. Pope, *The Iliad of Homer,* ed. Maynard Mack (London: Methuen, 1967). Chapman's *Homer*, op. cit.

23 Tytler's work followed closely after the publication in 1789 of George Campbell's *The Four Gospels*, of which Vol. I contains a study of the theory and history of translations of the Scriptures. Tytler's *Essay* appears with a useful introductory article by J.F. Huntsman in *Amsterdam Classics in Linguistics* vol. 13 (Amsterdam: John Benjamins B.V., 1978).

24 S.T. Coleridge, 'On Poesy and Art', *Biographia Literaria*, II (Oxford: Clarenden Press, 1907).

25 Paul van Tieghem, *Le Romantisme dans la littérature européenne* (Paris: Albin Michel, 1948).

26 Percy Bysshe Shelley, *The Defence of Poesy,* in *Complete Works*, V (London: Ernest Benn, 1965), pp. 109–43.

27 F.W. Newman, *Homeric Translation in Theory and Practice,* 1861 in *Essays by Matthew Arnold* (London: Oxford University Press, 1914), pp. 313–77.

28 G.A. Simcox, review in *Academy* II, Aug. 1890, pp. 278–9. This quotation, together with the comment by Oscar Wilde are taken from *William Morris. The Critical Heritage,* ed. P. Faulkner (London: Routledge & Kegan Paul, 1973).

29 W. Morris, *The Aeneid* VI (Boston: Roberts Bros., 1876), p. 146.

30 Thomas Carlyle, 'The State of German Literature' in *Critical and Miscellaneous Essays,* Vol. I (London: Chapman and Hall, 1905, p. 55).

31 Dante Gabriel Rossetti, Preface to his translations of Early Italian Poets, *Poems and Translations 1850–1870* (London: Oxford University Press, 1968), pp. 175–9.

32 Matthew Arnold, *On Translating Homer,* Lecture I, in *Essays by Matthew Arnold,* op. cit., p. 247.

33 Henry Wadsworth Longfellow, quoted in William J. De Sua, *Dante into English* (Chapel Hill: University of North Carolina Press, 1964), p. 65.

34 J.M. Cohen, *English Translators and Translations* (London: Longmans, Green and Co. pub. for The British Council and the National Book League, 1962), p. 24.

35 George Steiner, op. cit., p. 334.

36 R. Borchardt, *Dante und Deutscher Dante* (1908), reprinted in Lefevere, op. cit., p. 109.

37 James Holmes, José Lambert and Raymond van den Broeck (eds), *Literature and Translation* (Louvain: ACCO, 1978), p. VIII. The Preface to this volume describes Professor McFarlane's paper as a 'guiding principle'. The paper appeared in *Durham University Journal,* XLV, 1952–3, pp. 77–93.

38 George Steiner, op. cit., p. 269.

39 Maria Corti, *An Introduction to Literary Semiotics,* transl. M. Bogat and A. Mandelbaum (Bloomington and London: Indiana University Press, 1978).

40 Carlo Emilio Gadda, *In meditazione milanese* (Turin: Einaudi, 1974), p. 229.

3 Specific problems of literary translation

1 Anne Cluysenaar, *Introduction to Literary Stylistics* (London: Batsford, 1976), p. 49.

2 Robert Scholes, *Structuralism in Literature* (New Haven:

Yale University Press, 1974), p. 10.

3 Jurí Lotman, *Struktura Khudozhestvennogo Teksta* (Moscow: Iskusstvo, 1970) tr. *La struttura del testo poetico* (Milan: Musia, 1972).

4 Pablo Neruda, *Splendor and Death of Joaquín Murieta,* tr. Ben Belitt, (New York: Farrar, Strauss & Giroux, 1972).

5 Roland Barthes, *S/Z* (London: Cape, 1974).

6 Julia Kristeva, *Le texte du roman* (The Hague and Paris: Mouton, 1970).

7 Maria Corti, *An Introduction to Literary Semiotics* (Bloomington and London: Indiana University Press, 1978), p. 145.

8 See, for example Burton Raffel, *The Forked Tongue: A Study of the Translation Process* (The Hague: Mouton, 1971); C. Day Lewis, *On Translating Poetry* (Abingdon-on-Thames: Abbey Press, 1970); William de Sua, *Dante into English* (Chapel Hill: University of North Carolina Press, 1964); Paul Selver, *The Art of Translating Poetry* (London: Jon Baker, 1966).

9 André Lefevere, *Translating Poetry, Seven Strategies and a Blueprint* (Amsterdam: Van Gorcum, 1975).

10 Anton Popovič, 'The Concept of "Shift of Expression" in Translation Analysis' in James Holmes (ed.), *The Nature of Translation* (The Hague and Paris: Mouton, 1970).

11 J.P. Sullivan, 'The Poet as Translator – Ezra Pound and Sextus Propertius', *The Kenyon Review,* XXIII(3), Summer, 1961, pp. 462–82.

12 Professor W.G. Hale was a leading anti-Pound campaigner, whose virulent attacks on Pound's translation were at the centre of a lengthy debate on the nature of 'fidelity'.

13 Popovič distinguishes five types of shift:
   (a) *Constitutive shift*, that takes place inevitably due to differences between the two language systems.
   (b) *Generic shift,* described as 'a type of topical shift that implies a change in constitutive features of the text as a literary genre'.

(c) *Individual shift*, 'a system of individual deviations motivated by the translator's expressive propensities and his subjective idiolect'.

(d) *Negative shift*, where there has been a misunderstanding in the translation.

(e) *Topical shift*, where a difference in the topical facts between SL and TL versions is due to the use of different denotations. Popovič goes on to point out that this kind of shift can occur when connotation is favoured to the detriment of denotation.

14 Popovič, op. cit., p. 49.

15 Michael Rifaterre, *Semiotics of Poetry* (Bloomington and London: Indiana University Press, 1978), p. 166.

16 Tr. R.K. Gordon, *Anglo-Saxon Poetry* (London: Dent, 1926).

17 James Holmes, 'Forms of Verse Translation and the Translation of Verse Form', in James Holmes (ed.), *The Nature of Translation* (The Hague and Paris: Mouton, 1970).

18 Terry Eagleton, 'Translation and Transformation', *Stand*, 19(3), pp. 72–7.

19 Roman Ingarden, *The Literary Work of Art* (Evanston: The Northwestern University Press, 1973).

20 Wolfgang Iser, *The Implied Reader* (Baltimore and London: The Johns Hopkins Press, 1974), p. 277.

21 Hilaire Belloc, *On Translation* (Oxford: The Clarendon Press, 1931).

22 Alexandra Kollontai, *Love of Worker Bees*, tr. Cathy Porter (London: Virago, 1977), p. 226.

23 Boris Uspensky, *A Poetics of Composition* (Los Angeles: University of California Press, 1973).

24 Robert M. Adams, *Proteus, His Lies, His Truth* (New York: W.W. Norton, 1973), p. 12.

25 Jiří Levý, 'Translation as a Decision Process', *To Honour Roman Jakobson III* (The Hague: Mouton, 1967), pp. 1171–82.

26 Anne Ubersfeld, *Lire le théâtre* (Paris: Editions Sociales,

1978), pp. 15–16. See also Keir Elam, *Semiotics of Theatre and Drama* (London: Methuen, 1980).

27 Jiří Veltrusky, *Drama as Literature* (Lisse: Peter de Ridder Press, 1977), p. 10.

28 Robert Corrigan, 'Translating for Actors', in W. Arrowsmith and R. Shattuck (eds), *The Craft and Context of Translation* (Austin: University of Texas Press), 1961.

29 Peter Bogatyrev, 'Les signes du théâtre', *Poètique*, VIII, 1971, pp. 517–30.

30 Susan Bassnétt-McGuire, 'Translating Spatial Poetry: An Examination of Theatre Texts in Performance', in James Holmes, José Lambert and Raymond van den Broeck (eds), *Literature and Translation* (Louvain: ACCO, 1978), pp. 161–80.

31 Jean-Louis Barrault, *Phèdre de Jean Racine, mise en scène et commentaires* (Paris: Editions du Seuil, 1946).

32 James Holmes, 'Describing Literary Translations: Models and Methods', in James Holmes, José Lambert and Raymond van den Broeck (eds), *Literature and Translation* (Louvaine: ACCO, 1978).

33 T. Kowzan, *Littérature et Spectacle* (The Hague and Paris: Mouton, 1975).

34 It should be noted that gestural directions within the text are quite distinct from stage directions. However, as recent work in the semiotics of play texts has shown, there is a case for seeing the stage directions of some playwrights (e.g. Pirandello, Shaw, Wesker) as units of *narrative*, where a clearly distinguishable voice can be discerned.

Conclusion

1 R. Jakobson, 'On Linguistic Aspects of Translation', in R.A. Browes (ed.), *On Translation* (Cambridge, Mass.: Harvard University Press, 1959), p. 234.

SELECT BIBLIOGRAPHY

I N drawing up suggestions for further reading I have only
included those texts available in English. Details of useful
non-English language texts are given in notes to each
Section. I have also indicated below those texts that contain
comprehensive bibliographies.

Some English texts have not been included, on the grounds
that although they purport to be studies of translation, they
contain only subjective random observations on problems
encountered in the translation process and do not contribute
to the establishment of a critical discipline of Translation
Studies.

General introductory reading

ARROWSMITH, W. and SHATTUCK, R. (eds), *The Craft and
Context of Translation* (Austin: University of Texas Press,
1961). A useful collection of essays, dealing with general
and specific issues. Contained in the volume are two studies
of theatre translation, Peter Arnott on 'Translating the
Greeks' and Robert Corrigan on 'Translating for Actors'.

BROWER, REUBEN (ed.), *On Translation* (Cambridge, Mass.:
Harvard University Press, 1959). This collection of essays

is still one of the most useful anthologies in English, and
includes chapters on diverse aspects of translation. There
are chapters on Bible translation, on automatic translation
and, most importantly, the volume also contains Roman
Jakobson's 'On Linguistic Aspects of Translation'. Reuben
Brower is also editor of a volume entitled *Mirror on Mirror*,
published by Harvard in 1974, in which the discussion of
translation is extended outwards to include essays on imitation and parody.

SAVORY, THEODORE, *The Art of Translation* (London: Cape,
1957). The author of this book approaches Translation
Studies from the viewpoint of traditional liberal humanism.
Translation is perceived as a means of breaking down
communication barriers and the discussion remains on a
very unsystematic level.

STEINER, GEORGE, *After Babel: Aspects of Language and
Translation* (London: Oxford University Press, 1975). This
book covers a wide area and is particularly helpful in discussing the question of multilingualism and translation. Its
weakness lies in its pragmatism, which divorces it from so
much of the ongoing work in Translation Studies. The
bibliography is organized chronologically, beginning with
Schleiermacher's essay of 1813.

General translation theory

CATFORD, J.C., *A Linguistic Theory of Translation: An Essay
in Applied Linguistics* (London: Oxford University Press,
1965). This short study contains some insights into the
translation process viewed from a particular angle. Its chief
defect is that its author approaches the subject via a discussion of general linguistic theory and consequently translation is studied not as a discipline in its own right but as a way
of exemplifying aspects of applied linguistics.

GUENTHNER, F. and GUENTHNER-REUTTER, M. (eds), *Meaning and Translation. Philosophical and Linguistic
Approaches* (London: Duckworth, 1978).

LAWENDOWSKI, B.P., 'On Semiotic Aspects of Translation' in T. Sebeok (ed.), *Sight, Sound and Sense* (Bloomington: Indiana University Press, 1978), pp. 264–82.

LEVÝ, JIŘÍ, 'The Translation of Verbal Art', in L. Matejka and I.R. Titunik (eds), *Semiotics of Art* (Cambridge, Mass.: MIT Press, 1976), pp. 218–27.

LUDSKANOV, A., 'A Semiotic Approach to the Theory of Translation', *Language Sciences*, 35, April 1975, pp. 5–8.

McFARLANE, J., 'Modes of Translation', *Durham University Journal*, 14, 1953, pp. 77–93.

NEWMARK, P., 'Twenty-three Restricted Rules of Translation', *The Incorporated Linguist*, 12(1), 1973, pp. 9–15.

NIDA, E., *Towards a Science of Translating* (Leiden: E.J. Brill, 1964). An extremely helpful book, invaluable for the student of translation, it also contains an extensive bibliography on the specific question of Bible Translation.

NIDA, E. and TABER, C., *The Theory and Practice of Translation* (Leiden: E.J. Brill, 1969).

History of translation theory

COHEN, J.M., *English Translators and Translations* (London: Longmans, pub. for the British Council and the National Book League, 1962).

JACOBSEN, ERIC, *Translation: A Traditional Craft* (Copenhagen: Nordisk Forlag, 1958). This book contains much interesting information about the function of translation within the terms of medieval rhetorical tradition, but, as the author states in the introduction, avoids as far as possible discussion of the general theory and principles of translation.

KELLY, L.G., *The True Interpreter: A History of Translation Theory and Practice in the West* (Oxford: Blackwell, 1979).

LEFEVERE, ANDRÉ (ed.), *Translating Literature: The German Tradition from Luther to Rosenzweig* (Amsterdam and Assen: Van Gorcum, 1977). A selection of writings on translation by major German translators, organized to give an overview of changing attitudes to translation.

MATTIESSON, F.O., *Translation: An Elizabethan Art* (Cambridge, Mass.: Harvard University Press, 1931). A useful, but unsystematic, analysis of the work of four major Elizabethan translators, Hoby, North, Florio and Philemon Holland.

STEINER, T.R., *English Translation Theory, 1650–1800* (Amsterdam and Assen: Van Gorcum, 1975). This volume is particularly helpful in that it contains a long critical essay on the changing pattern of English translation theory from 1650–1800 and an anthology of selected writings on translation from the same period.

Literary translation theory

ADAMS, R., *Proteus, His Lies, His Truth: Discussions on Literary Translation* (New York: W.H. Norton, 1973). A highly idiosyncratic book, but which contains some useful examples of specific problems of literary translation.

ARNOLD, MATTHEW, 'On Translating Homer', *Essays by Matthew Arnold* (London: Oxford University Press, 1914). This volume also contains F.W. Newman's attack on Arnold's theory of translation, 'Homeric Translation in Theory and Practice'.

BEAUGRANDE, ROBERT de, *Factors in a Theory of Poetic Translating* (Amsterdam and Assen: Van Gorcum, 1978).

BELLOC, HILAIRE, *On Translation* (Oxford: The Clarendon Press, 1931).

DAVIE, DONALD, *Poetry in Translation* (Milton Keynes: The Open University Press, 1975).

DAY LEWIS, C., *On Translating Poetry* (Abingdon-on-Thames: Abbey Press, 1970).

EAGLETON, TERRY, 'Translation and Transformation', *Stand*, XIX(3), 1977, pp. 72–7.

HOLMES, JAMES (ed.), *The Nature of Translation: Essays on the Theory and Practice of Literary Translation* (The Hague: Mouton, 1970). This volume contains a number of important chapters, in particular J. Holmes' 'Forms of Verse Translation and the Translation of Verse Form' and Anton Popovič's 'The Concept of "Shift of Expression" in Translation Analysis'.

HOLMES, J., LAMBERT, J. and LEFEVERE, A. (eds), *Literature and Translation* (Louvain: ACCO, 1978). This volume contains the papers read at the colloquium on Literature and Translation held at the Catholic University of Leuven in 1976, together with a statement on the establishment of Translation Studies as a discipline. There is an extensive bibliography, though organized in a slightly clumsy manner, that gives details of texts on translation in English, French and German.

LEFEVERE, ANDRÉ, *Translating Poetry: Seven Strategies and a Blueprint* (Assen and Amsterdam: Van Gorcum, 1975). A very useful book that tackles the problem of establishing a methodology for translating poetry through an investigation of seven translations of a Latin text.

POPOVIČ, ANTON, *A Dictionary for the Analysis of Literary Translation* (Edmonton, Alberta: Department of Comparative Literature, University of Alberta, 1976).

POUND, EZRA, *Literary Essays* (London: Faber, 1954).

SELVER, PAUL, *The Art of Translating Poetry* (London: Jon Baker, 1966).

Periodicals

Articles on translation are spread through a wide range of journals, especially in the field of linguistics and comparative philology. Of those periodicals in English devoted exclusively to translation the most significant is *Babel,* the journal of the International Federation of Translators (FIT) (1955 –).

The defunct journal *Delos*, published by the University of Texas at Austin (1968–71) contains some valuable work on the theory and practice of translation.

Information on conferences, new publishing ventures, courses in establishments of higher education can be found in

TRANSST: An International Newsletter of Translation Studies, Amsterdam, Institute of General Literary Studies, University of Amsterdam.

APPENDIX

The original text of *The Seafarer*

Mæg ic be me sylfum   soðgied wrecan,
siþas secgan,   hu ic geswincdagum
earfoðhwile   oft þrowade,
bitre breostceare   gebiden hæbbe,
5   gecunnad in ceole   cearselda fela,
atol yþa gewealc,   þær mec oft bigeat
nearo nihtwaco   æt nacan stefnan,
þonne he be clifum cnossað.   Calde geþrungen
wæron mine fet,   forste gebunden,
10   caldum clommum,   þær þa ceare seofedun
hat ymb heortan;   hungor innan slat
merewerges mod.   Þæt se mon ne wat
þe him on foldan   fægrost limpeð,
hu ic earmcearig   iscealdne sæ
15   winter wunade   wræccan lastum,
winemægum bidroren,
bihongen hrimgicelum;   hægl scurum fleag.
    Þær ic ne gehyrde   butan hlimman sæ,
iscaldne wæg.   Hwilum ylfete song
20   dyde ic me to gomene,   ganetes hleoþor
ond huilpan sweg   fore hleahtor wera,
mæw singende   fore medodrince.
Stormas þær stanclifu beotan,   þær him stearn oncwæð
isigfeþera;   ful oft þæt earn bigeal,
25   urigfeþra;   nænig hleomæga
feasceaftig ferð   frefran meahte.

Forþon him gelyfeð lyt,   se þe ah lifes wyn
gebiden in burgum,   bealosiþa hwon,
wlonc ond wingal,   hu ic werig oft
30 in brimlade   bidan sceolde.
Nap nihtscua,   norþan sniwde,
hrim hrusan bond,   hægl feol on eorþan,
corna caldast.   Forþon cnyssað nu
heortan geþohtas,   þæt ic hean streamas,
35 sealtyþa gelac   sylf cunnige;
monað modes lust   mæla gehwylce
ferð to feran,   þæt ic feor heonan
elþeodigra   eard gesece.
Forþon nis þæs modwlonc   mon ofer eorþan,
40 ne his gifena þæs god,   ne in geoguþe to þæs hwæt,
ne in his dædum to þæs deor,   ne him his dryhten to þæs hold,
þæt he a his sæfore   sorge næbbe,
to hwon hine Dryhten   gedon wille.
Ne biþ him to hearpan hyge   ne to hringþege,
45 ne to wife wyn   ne to worulde hyht,
ne ymbe owiht elles   nefne ymb yða gewealc;
ac a hafað longunge   se þe on lagu fundað.
Bearwas blostmum nimað,   byrig fægriað,
wongas wlitigað,   woruld onetteð;
50 ealle þa gemoniað   modes fusne
sefan to siþe,   þam þe swa þenceð
on flodwegas   feor gewitan.
Swylce geac monað   geomran reorde,
singeð sumeres weard,   sorge beodeð
55 bitter in breosthord.   Þæt se beorn se wat,
esteadig secg,   hwæt þa sume dreogað
þe þa wræclastas   widost lecgað.
     Forþon nu min hyge hweorfeð   ofer hreþerlocan,
min modsefa   mid mereflode,
60 ofer hwæles eþel   hweorfeð wide,
eorþan sceatas,   cymeð eft to me
gifre ond grædig;   gielleð anfloga,
hweteð on hwælweg   hreþer unwearnum,
ofer holma gelagu.
                    Forþon me hatran sind
65 Dryhtnes dreamas   þonne þis deade lif,
læne on londe.   Ic gelyfe no
þæt him eorðwelan   ece stondað.

APPENDIX 155

Simle þreora sum   þinga gehwylce
ær his tid aga   to tweon weorþeð:
70 adl oþþe yldo   oþþe ecghete
fægum fromweardum   feorh oðþringeð.
Forþon þæt bið eorla gehwam   æftercweþendra
lof lifgendra   lastworda betst,
þæt he gewyrce   ær he on weg scyle,
75 fremum on foldan   wið feonda niþ,
deorum dædum   deofle togeanes,
þæt hine ælda bearn   æfter hergen,
ond his lof siþþan   lifge mid englum
awa to ealdre,   ecan lifes blæd,
80 dream mid dugeþum.
                    Dagas sind gewitene,
ealle onmedlan   eorþan rices.
Nearon nu cyningas   ne caseras
ne goldgiefan   swylce iu wæron,
þonne hi mæst mid him   mærþa gefremedon
85 ond on dryhtlicestum   dome lifdon.
Gedroren is þeos duguð eal,   dreamas sind gewitene;
wuniað þa wacran   ond þas woruld healdaþ,
brucað þurh bisgo.   Blæd is gehnæged,
eorþan indryhto   ealdað ond searað,
90 swa nu monna gehwylc   geond middangeard.
Yldo him on fareð,   onsyn blacað,
gomelfeax gnornað, wat his iuwine,
æþelinga bearn   eorþan forgiefene.
Ne mæg him þonne se flæschoma,   þonne him þæt feorg losað,
95 ne swete forswelgan   ne sar gefelan,
ne hond onhreran   ne mid hyge þencan.
Þeah þe græf wille   golde stregan
broþor his geborenum,   byrgan be deadum
maþmum mislicum,   þæt hine mid wille,
100 ne mæg þære sawle   þe biþ synna ful
gold to geoce   for Godes egsan,
þonne he hit ær hydeð   þenden he her leofað.
        Micel biþ se Meotudes egsa,   forþon hi seo molde oncyrreð;
se gestaþelade   stiþe grundas,
105 eorþan sceatas   ond uprodor.
Dol biþ se þe him his Dryhten ne ondrædeþ;   cymeð him se deað unþinged.
Eadig bið se þe eaþmod leofaþ;   cymeð him seo ar of heofonum.
Meotod him þæt mod gestaþelað,   forþon he in his meahte
                                    gelyfeð.

INDEX

Adams, R., 119, 145
adaptation, 79
Alfred, 50, 51, 52, 141
archaism/-izing/-ization in translation, 10, 68, 69, 72, 73, 101
Arnold, M., 9, 69, 70, 72, 143
artificial language, 66

Bacon, R., 52
Barrault, J.L., 124, 146
Barthes, R., 79, 117, 144
du Bellay, J., 56
Belitt, B., 78, 123, 124, 144
Belloc, H., 2, 74, 116, 117, 119, 136, 145
Benjamin, W., 75
Blake, W., 65
blank verse translation, 79
Bogatyrev, P., 122, 123, 146
Borchardt, R., 72, 73, 143
Boreck, R. van den, 26, 136, 139

Carlyle, T., 67, 68, 69, 143
Cary, E., 55, 142
Catford, J.C., 5, 24, 32, 33, 34, 35, 137, 139
Catullus, 9, 81, 84–91, 104, 109
Chapman, G., 10, 54, 55, 56, 61, 62, 142

Chaucer, G., 41, 53
Chomsky, N., 36, 102
Cicero, 40, 42–4, 46, 73, 140, 141
Cluysenaar, A., 76, 77, 82, 143
Cohen, J.M., 72, 73, 143
Coleridge, S.T., 64, 142
Copley, F. (translator of Catullus), 85, 88–9, 104
Corrigan, R., 122, 146
Corti, M., 75, 80, 83, 143
Coverdale's Bible, 48, 49
Cowley, A., 59, 60, 142
Cowper, W., 41
Creagh, P. (translator of Ungaretti), 102–3
creative transposition, 15
cultural untranslatability, 32, 34

Dagut, M.B., 24, 139
Dante, A., 41, 52, 53, 65, 70, 72, 144
Darbelnet, J.L. and Vinay, J.P., 34, 140
David, G. and Mossbacher, E. (translators of Silone), 112–14
Day Lewis, C., 73, 77, 144
decoding and recoding, 16–38
Denham, Sir J., 41, 59, 142

Descartes, R., 58
Dolet, E., 54–6
Dryden, J., 60, 63, 74, 131, 142
Durišin, D., 28
dynamic equivalence, 26

Eagleton, T., 104, 145
Erasmus, D., 48, 69, 141
equivalence, 10, 15, 18, 23, 24, 26, 27, 28, 29, 37, 119
evaluation of translations, 8–10

Firth, J.R., 21, 138
Fischbach, H., 136, 137
Fitzgerald, E., 3, 70–2, 137
Florio, J., 41
Fokkema, D.W., 139
Folena, G., 52, 53, 141
formal equivalence, 26
Frenz, H., 4, 137

Gadda, C.E., 75, 143
gestural patterning/text/under-structure, 123, 124, 131
Goethe, J.W. von, 41, 62–4, 66
Gottsched, J.C., 41
Graves, R., 73

Harrison, T. (translator of Racine), 126–32
hierarchy of correspondences, 126
Hjelmslev, L., 36
Hoby, Sir T., 41
Hölderlin, F., 74
Holland, P., 41, 57, 58
Holmes, J., 28, 126, 134, 136, 139, 145, 146
Horace, 40, 43–4, 52, 73, 141
horizontal (translation), 52–3

imitatio, 53
Ingarden, R., 114–15
influence (study of), 7, 42
interlingual translation, 14, 80
interlingual transposition, 15, 18
interpretation, 82
intersemiotic translation, 14
intertextuality, 79, 104, 117
intralingual translation, 14–15
intralingual transposition, 15

invariant, invariant core, 18, 22, 26–7, 87
Iser, W., 114–15, 145

Jacobsen, E., 4, 43, 137, 140–1
Jakobson, R., 5, 14, 15, 18, 90, 135, 138, 146
Johnson, Dr S., 61
Jonson, B., 85–9, 109

Kennedy, C.W. (translator of The Seafarer), 91–3, 96–100
King James Bible, 50
Knyghton, the Chronicler, 47
Kollontai, A., 118, 145
Kowzan, T., 131, 146
Kristeva, J., 79, 144

Larbaud, V., 40, 73, 75
Lawendowski, B., 35, 40
Lefevere, A., 1, 7, 9, 37, 41, 81, 82, 134, 136, 137, 140, 144
Levý, J., 5, 22, 36, 119, 137, 140, 145
Lindisfarne Gospels, 50
linguistic equivalence, 8, 25
linguistic untranslatability, 6, 8, 32, 34
literal translation, 81
Longfellow, W., 70, 100, 143
Longinus, 45, 141
loss and gain in translation, 30
Lotman, J., 14, 29, 33, 41, 77–8, 138–40, 144
Lowell, R. (translator of Racine), 127–32
Lowe-Porter, H.T. (translator of Mann), 110–12
Ludskanov, A., 18, 90, 138
Luther, M., 41, 48–9, 62, 74, 141

McFarlane, J., 74, 143
MacKenna, N., 74
Mallarmé, S., 24, 66
Mann, T. (The Magic Mountain), 110–12, 118
Marris, Sir W. (translator of Catullus), 84, 87–8
Mattiesson, F.O., 41, 42, 56, 140

metrical translation, 80
modernization, 101
Morris, W., 67, 68, 100–1, 143
Moscow Linguistic Circle, 36
Mounin, G., 15, 35, 36, 138, 140
Mukařovsky, J., 5, 29

negative shift, 115, 139, 145
Neubert, A., 23, 25–7, 29, 139
Newman, F., 9, 67, 72, 137, 142
Nietzsche, F.W., 75
Nida, E., 16–18, 21, 26, 30, 71, 137, 138, 141
North, Sir T., 41, 56
Novalis, 74

ostranenie, 103

paradigmatic equivalence, 25
paralinguistic systems, 131
Paz, O., 38, 79, 139
performance-oriented translation, 131
Petrarch, 41, 56–7, 105–9
Phillips, A., 125–6
Phillips, J.B., 26
phonemic translation, 81
Pierce, C.S., 27, 139
playability, 122, 125
poetry into prose, 81
Pope, A., 10, 61, 62, 142
Popovič, A., 5, 25–6, 29, 32, 34–5, 82–3, 87, 115, 134, 137–8, 144
Porter, C., 118, 145
Pound, E., 74–5, 82–3, 93–100, 104
Prague Linguistic Circle, 5, 28, 36
Prochazka, 5
Purvey, J., 46–7

Quadrivium, 51
Quine, W.V., 75
Quintilian, 51–3
Quirk, R., 5, 137

Rabelais, F., 41
Racine, J., 123–32
reader-oriented translation, 131
Rieu, E.V., 26

Rifaterre, M., 90, 145
Rosenzweig, F., 41, 75
Rossetti, D.G., 3, 67–8, 71, 137, 143
Russian Formalism, 5, 28, 103

St Jerome, 46
Sapir, E., 13–14, 138
Saussure, F., 18, 36, 138
Savory, T., 4, 137
Schlegel, A.W., 41, 65
Schlegel, F., 41, 65
Schlegel-Tieck translations of Shakespeare, 65
Schleiermacher, F.E.D., 41, 67, 69, 71, 75
Scholes, R., 77, 143
Seafarer, The, 91–9
semantic equivalence, 120
semantic relationships, 19
semiotics, 13
semiotic category, 27, 29
semiotic transformation, 18, 24, 90
sense for sense translation, 39, 42, 44, 53, 60
separate translation language, 67
Shelley, P.B., 41, 64, 66, 67, 75, 142
shift of expression, 83, 89, 104
Shukman, A., 139
significations, 15, 33
Silone (*Fontamara*), 112–14, 118
spirit of original, 55, 60, 61
stylistic equivalence, 25
Steiner, G., 40, 58, 72–5, 140, 142, 143
Steiner, T.R., 41, 140
Surrey, H.H., Earl of (translator of Petrarch), 30, 56, 106–9

textual equivalence, 25
Tieghem, P. van, 64, 142
Tomlinson, C. (translator of Ungaretti), 102–3
transformations, 27
translation-reading, 104
translation units, 117
Trevisa, J. of, 53
Trivium, 51
Tyndale, W., 47–8

Tytler, A.F., 3, 40, 63, 142

Ubersfeld, A., 120, 121, 145
Ungaretti, G. (*Un'altra notte*),
    101–4
untranslatability, 6, 10, 22, 32,
    34–5, 66
Uspensky, B., 119, 138, 140, 145

Valéry, P., 77
Veltrusky, J., 121, 146
verdeutschen, 49
versions, 79, 82, 100
vertical translation, 52–3

Vinay, J.P. and Darbelnet, J.L., 34
Volosinov, V., 5
Voss, J.H., 63

Webb, T., 41, 66, 75, 140
Whorf, B.L., 14, 30, 31, 140
Wieland, C.M., 62
Wilde, O., 67
word for word translation, 39, 42,
    44, 60
Wyatt, Sir T. (translator of
    Petrarch), 30, 56–7, 105–9
Wycliffe, J., 46
Wycliffite Bible, 46–7